W9-BHB-379

Writing From The Inside Out

WRITING FROM THE INSIDE OUT

by Charlotte Edwards

Writer's Digest Books

Cincinnati, Ohio

Writing from the Inside Out. Copyright 1984 by Charlotte Edwards. Printed and bound in the United States of America. All rights reserved. No part of this book may be reproduced in any form or by any electronic or mechanical means including information storage and retrieval systems without permission in writing from the publisher, except by a reviewer who may quote brief passages in a review. Published by Writer's Digest Books, 9933 Alliance Road, Cincinnati, OH 45242. First edition.

Library of Congress Cataloging in Publication Data

Edwards, Charlotte, 1907-
    Writing from the inside out.

    Includes index.
    1. Authorship. 2. Creative writing. I. Title.
PN187.E36 1984   808   83-27431
ISBN 0-89879-130-8

Design by Charleen Catt Lyon

Contents

Foreword

From the moment the first words were set on paper there have been all kinds of writing in the world. Actually, of course, there was writing before paper as we know it—hieroglyphics on pyramid walls, lost languages carved into stone, paintings in caves.

Human beings have tried to "tell it like it is" for a very long while. They've been reluctant to leave this life without also leaving footprints, though they might be blown by the wind, or lost in translation.

People have reported the news and that is one kind of writing. As time passes, this news becomes *history.*

People have also tried to reach out long fingers beyond straight reporting. They've turned words into living people with characters on a stage. As technology has advanced, this stage playing has moved on to screens of all kinds—some in our homes, some in public places—and has become a powerful influence in directing public opinion and mores.

This kind of writing is called *drama.*

Humans have attempted to understand the universe, the people within it; reaching upward and outward toward the stars and to new frontiers of every kind. They've tried to explain in words why they're here in the first place, where they're going, why they feel the way they do.

This is *philosophy.*

People have tried, too, over the years, to set within the realms of imagination some of the true situations they see about them in novels, in short stories.

This is *fiction.*

Then, beginning to explore within themselves, they've written—short or long—the odd thoughts, recollections, morals, and personal observations of daily living, collecting them like varied seashells from the ocean of their world. This is nonfiction and there are many types.

For instance, as events shape people through pain or grief or hard-won faith, they've sought to put together sentences which may be of help to others in times of stress, or in seeking happiness or in God-searching.

This is *inspirational*.

Some people, blessed with a light touch, a rare and delicious view of man's plight on earth, see every happening and occasionally life itself, as ridiculous. Even the direst circumstances strike them as funny.

This is *humor*.

And others, with the humorous approach turned slightly sour or even bitter, often have a needle or a knife hidden in their phrases.

This is *satire*.

Lastly, there is the precise and delicate search for words that somehow can portray the reaching beyond our most inner selves to color and add magic to the outside world. Sometimes it rhymes; many times it doesn't. But always it finds a fragment of beauty to polish.

This is *poetry*.

All of these—and any others which may be added to them from bedtime stories to doctoral dissertations—bear the seed of creative writing. To create, in its most basic form, means to make something where nothing was before—to give birth—to take raw materials and mold them together into some sort of a whole.

Sometimes it seems, during the long, hard years of living that each of us goes through, that words, either to be read, or to be put on a page by us, are stumbling blocks—hurdles to catch our heels or traps into which we fall. We were never comfortable with them in the first place, and most of them lead, in an erratic path, to questions on quizzes or letters to friends, a club book review, or even an obituary for a loved one. We get pretty weary of words.

But this doesn't have to be so.

Most of us talk well enough; some very well indeed. But average people get by with a sort of jargon. The slang of the day. The phrases of simple social exchange. A working vocabulary for the area in which they either study or earn their living.

But there are many more sentences hidden in the corners of our minds and mouths than we ever use.

The educated world of today is articulate in a way no other

generation has been. It's filled with phrases, slogans, labels, shortcuts, abbreviations, warmed-over arguments from books half-read and ideas half-digested. The creative, in many fields, has been lost in the easy acquirement of slang—thoughtless labels and superficial phrases.

The creative, in writing, in art, in music, is still there, however—hidden and a little shy—but there to be discovered if you try. It's an expanding experience, more psychedelic than any drug, more exciting than any outward adventure, more soothing than any tranquilizer.

It's a journey, too, creative writing. A journey to an unknown destination through secret tunnels of the mind, into a blinding sort of light and scenery undreamed of.

This expansion, this journey, lies in learning to write from the hidden recesses of your own self, exploring as you go, ending up no one knows where. It's learning to write from the inside out.

And it is done with words. Words come alive with explorations, just as rivers and mountains and seas and new country once revealed themselves to the European explorers who discovered America.

This is an age of the "identity crisis," an age of alienation, when humans, young and old, male and female, live in a cocoon of loneliness that can't seem to be penetrated by any hopes we have at our command. This is an age of anxieties about the role of breadwinner, parenting, cancer, the quality of life and the quality of the air we breathe and the soil that bears our food. This is the age of a mushroom future. The present becomes of paramount importance when the long thoughts of tomorrow are cut off short. The impersonal and the insecure, the confused and uncertain, the violent and hating, make this cocoon thicker.

Learning to use words to express what you are thinking and feeling, discovering you're thinking and feeling them in the first place, can be the spear that breaks the cocoon of loneliness.

The purpose of this book is to help you take this journey, first to inner space, and then outward, aware and alive as you have not been before. It's also my hope that you'll learn to manage words instead of having words manage you.

But this book was written with a deeper hope—that what I have *lived*, from the inside out, what I have learned of writing from this inner resource, will spark you to effort, to accomplishment, to a richness of experience.

Author's Note

Before you read *Writing from the Inside Out*, let me make a few suggestions about the purpose and the method of using this book.

It is designed and created for *anybody* who wants to write almost *anything*. If your interest is fiction, it is pointed in that direction. If nonfiction intrigues you this area is covered also. Playwriting and poetry are left to books that concentrate on them (although the attitudes in this book could well be applied to both fields).

Writing from the Inside Out may be effectively used by a teacher in a regular classroom. But it's also slanted for those who are learning on their own—the housewife at the kitchen table after the kids are in bed, the businessman who wants to escape a structured life by working on The Great American Novel in whatever free time he can manage, or the many people in evening classes, large or small, who are expressing their lives and experiences on paper.

May I suggest also that it's all right to scan through the book at first. But if you plan to work either on your own by studying it, or in any kind of class, it's vital that you *take your time*. In a classroom, of course, the teacher will set the pace, give you the go-ahead when it's suitable, and restrain you when it isn't. But some of the chapters take from four to six weeks to do properly. Others, more general, can march by smartly. But it's very important that every assignment be understood well, done fully and carefully. Sometimes, more than one of a kind should be done.

This way you will become fluent with each step before moving on to the next one.

Good luck!

CHAPTER 1

It Isn't Just the Words

If you write a great deal, and some of it's been published, people have quite a few things to say to you, one way or another. After all, words (and by extension, writing) belong to all of us. Didn't we learn to read in the first grade? This automatically makes any regular reader of an evening newspaper an authority on the medium with which the writer works. And sometimes he can cut as well as praise. This is not true of art, or music, or even the creative acts of building, wiring, or painting a house. What we don't know about we usually have a hearty respect for.

THE ARMCHAIR CRITIC

But when a piece of writing is in the newspaper, a magazine or a book, people approach you. They have comments. Do they ever have comments!

No matter how simple your story (or article or essay or poem), the reader usually holds definite opinions. He is eager to share them. Also, as a rule, he or she plans to "do some of those little things for the magazines" or "write a Great American Novel" just as soon as he or she has "a few minutes' free time." This reaction is human, expected, and all right. That reader knows as many words as you do, and thinks that settles the matter.

And he's at least partially right. In the beginning was the Word. That, of course, comes from the Bible. Without being the least blasphemous, it's also true of people who write, who want to write, who try to write, or who dream of writing—and never do.

The word entrances them all. They love the flow of a phrase, the rhythmic pattern of a sentence, the smooth movement from paragraph to paragraph. They are intelligent and critical of stories and books they read; they can tell a good one from a bad one, as people viewing paintings in a gallery say "I know what I like." The instinctive feeling for clarity of ideas and words is often theirs.

There is a danger here for you who are beginning. You can be deluded with the dream that if you know enough words and put them down in certain patterns, you will come up with something worth reading—and that it will be read! But this isn't necessarily an automatic, reflex action.

Most books on writing deal with the use of words. They analyze plots, call the hero and heroine definitive names, tell how to build to a climax, and unwind the whole thing. They serve a good purpose and teach us a lot. And, as together we explore the business of writing—as I take a sort of inventory of my own writing years—I sincerely hope that what I've learned in craft and skill and technique will be of help to you who are beginning.

However, there are limitations to studying this way; learning just the mechanics of putting words together in logical order is a very small part of being a writer. Almost anybody can learn to do those things. Almost anybody can learn to play the piano. Play it well, sometimes, even technically perfect—but without heart, without an inner nuance. We are not concerned with such here. Any book on writing can give you that much.

Being a writer, you see, goes beyond phraseology, beyond plot and counterplot and characters. Beyond protagonist and flashback, narration, and description. Beyond all of the definitions of writing terms, so easily discovered, along with all those hundreds of thousands of words, in any adequate dictionary.

In creative writing it isn't enough to dash off twenty or two hundred pages of copy, no matter how fluent, how flexible, or how colorful those pages may be. Not unless you have a good hold on a certain set of intangibles—and above all else, on yourself.

To use our piano analogy again. The audience, listening to a technically perfect pianist, hears the notes as they were written by the composer. Hears them in correct sequence, without mistakes. And comes away from the concert feeling unfulfilled, slightly empty in the ears.

Why is this? Because the pianist, concentrating on those notes, memorized and hard-won, is not himself part of the concerto, or sonata. He has withheld himself—or perhaps he is even barren of self. A mechnical master only.

So it is with writing those flexible, fluent pages. Not enough.

Before pencil can be touched to paper, or fingers to typewriter keys, there is the stage *before* the beginning, before the putting together of words, the many phrases, the ideas, the learning how-to. This is the most important stage of all. It's simple. It's complex. It's fascinating. It's dull. It's you, yourself!

It is an obvious fact, and one apt to be overlooked in this frantic world, that you lead two lives.

The first is the life of getting up in the morning, bathing, dressing, eating, going to school or to work, or to the supermarket. Eventually you eat again, study or watch TV, visit friends, go to a party or a game, and back to bed again. With small variations.

This—again obviously—is your external life. It sometimes absorbs the major portion of your conscious mind, particularly if you like what you're doing. It sometimes absorbs your emotions with those you love, causes you support, friends you enjoy. But it hardly ever absorbs *you*. The *you* of the second life.

THE HIDDEN YOU

This life has been with you always, of course. It's the hidden, secret, sweet or fearful life of your subconscious. It's never still. It's always moving, even when you sleep, transforming itself into dreams. From it come all of the colors which paint your world in tones that are yours alone, colors which make you different and special as a person. From it, too, come the accumulations and hodgepodge of everything you have ever thought or felt or hoped.

It is an overflowing basket of all the deeper emotions and ideas, and the sillier ones too, which you have never shared with anybody. As a matter of fact, most times you haven't even shared them with yourself, as any good psychiatrist would testify.

You know how it is. You are walking down the street and the automatic (or conditioned) part of your mind keeps your feet moving. Trained reflexes. The conscious part of your mind goes over the book you've read, the bills you have to pay, the dentist appointment, the score of the game, the conversation you had this morning.

Undercurrent to this mental housekeeping, though, is the subconscious. It is noting, in flashing pictures, the way the trees have blossomed or changed, the smell of the early morning, the sound of traffic, and hundreds of other impressions.

This is the secret *you* that will make you write. This inner world—untouched, untapped, dark as any well, shining as any star—is the *source of all writing*. No two leaves are the same. No two people are the same. You know this, acknowledge it, but you don't give it much attention.

Until you want to write. Then you must consider this fact very carefully.

The way each writer's *inner* self surfaces and floats in a specific direction, is the wonder that makes each person putting words to paper unique.

It's also what endows each person with something worthy of being recorded. There is not one life that wouldn't make a book—if it could be translated in depth, in language.

Somebody once said that there are no new ideas. Most likely this is true. But one thing is certain. Nobody—nobody in the whole of history or living today—has ever thought and felt about an idea in exactly the same way, with exactly the same perspective, as you do.

Hang on to this knowledge!

Now—it's a long hard journey from this inner world, filtered through mind and memory, out onto the blank white page. It's as difficult and dangerous and exciting—as anticipatory, as rewarding and sometimes as disappointing—as the birth of any child.

This journey is called "learning to write." No vocabulary, no dictionary full of words, can do it for you. Except this one vocabulary—the dictionary of *personal attitude* toward what is happening and what has happened to *you*. Everything that you remember and hold over the years. In viewpoint. Belief. Emotion. Intellect.

How do you begin to make this journey?

In a way, you start by packing for it, and you do that by checking to see what you have on hand to take with you.

Assess what you are at this moment, what you have in your hands and your heart and your mind that will make you open to suggestion, aware of your own person behind everything you study or learn. It's sort of like looking at yourself after a shower in a full-length mirror. Do you need to go on a diet or should you put on a few pounds? Are some areas of your body in need of exercise? Would a new haircut improve you?

You came into the world with a certain set of basics. No two basics are the same. The accent seems to be on one thing or another psychologically. But you can attain what you lack, if you can recognize it (and really want it enough). And what you *have*, you can extend.

As you start inventorying your tools for writing, try to be very honest. You need both the good and the bad, the dark and the shine in those cartons for your trip.

YOU ARE WHAT YOU FEEL

A writer can be born with a deftness in the word department, but it will do no good unless coupled with a sensitivity to people. This is a positive intangible, one which may be cultivated, although most authors seem to have it instinctively.

This sensitivity is a strange and lovely thing. It doesn't mean that you go through life "simply crazy" about everybody you meet. You're human, and some people rub you the wrong way—or are downright rough with you, and your emotions kick up.

It does mean, though, that you care about people. You stand, you listen, you observe, and you get outside of yourself. The first thing you know, you're inside the other guy. You don't condone how it is with him. You don't approve, maybe. But you don't disapprove, either. You're tolerant. You're compassionate. Because you *know* how it is with him. You have a feeling for the way life piles up on him, why he does what he does when he wants out from his troubles. You don't want to change him because if you did he wouldn't be the person he is, with his own integrity, his own completeness.

Sensitivity comes first then, the largest and most important piece of luggage for a writer. Either consciously or unconsciously, it must be practiced so that when it is strengthened, deepened, honed, it can lead naturally into the next big element necessary to writing.

THE UNIVERSAL MIND

You may be able to string words together with lightning speed, but if you have no comprehension of the meaning of universality, you'll have a tough time being a writer of anything except flip tales.

Universality is a sort of recognition of yourself in everybody and everybody in yourself. As a writer it gives you one of the most precious attributes—that of *reader identification*. Because if you can make your characters and situations universal, your reader will say, with delight, with self-pity, with humor, "That's me, all right! I've felt that way. I've thought that very thought."

You'll hear more and at length about these two great facets of writing—and of living, for that matter. But right now, let's see if I can give you an example of what I mean from my own memories.

I can remember one day, smart-alecky little mutt that I was, sitting on a streetcar going home from school. Kitty-corner from me was a woman. I guess she was just a girl. I'm not exactly doddering, but when I was in high school women didn't use much makeup. This girl had a snow white face with two almost perfect round circles of rouge in the middle of her cheeks. Her mouth was shiny with bright lipstick and looked swollen. Her hair was frizzy and yellow. Not gold, nor copper, not even brass. Just yellow.

I stared at her and some of my mother's vague intimations wandered through my head. I smoothed back my own clean braids and I let my unrouged mouth curl up. I don't know why. Something to do maybe. It was a long ride from downtown Central High to Kahkwa Park.

She turned her head and she caught my look. She caught it literally. Like a ballplayer gets a fast one in the stomach sometimes. Her swollen mouth opened a little, fishlike and hunting for air, and her eyelids went down. Under the too-white powder, deep red as the spots of rouge, her own color rose up and up until it looked as if it might set the frizzy sawdust hair on fire. She got off at the next stop.

"Well, she probably planned to get off anyhow," I told myself defiantly. "And she must have been a bad woman or she wouldn't have looked so guilty from my scorn."

But I felt awful about it. For five terrible minutes, until I reached my own stop, I *was* that girl. I was shabby with ten-cent jewelry and makeup to help me look prettier. I was hoping some nice man would see under it all and know that I could have fine sturdy babies and could keep a house so clean you could eat off the floor.

That's the first time I remember sensitivity. It didn't start there I'm sure, that feeling about people. But it's the time I remember first. It didn't last long because I couldn't stand being that girl for long and I was young. There were a lot of things that interested me. But over the years it has grown to that larger state of universality, as well as the rare quality of empathy, to be discussed in Chapter 6.

BELIEVE IN YOURSELF

You may be able to write descriptions in your sleep. But if you don't have faith in yourself you don't stand a chance of being a real writer.

This faith is a complex and violent thing. Complex because it is made up of so many small hurting things. And violent because you can be egotistically bursting with it one moment and punctured balloon flat with lack of it the next. It's never a quality that just coasts along, backed by your previous successes, or your family's righteous wrath if every golden word you write isn't instantly appreciated—or, conversely, your family's and your friends' criticisms and ribbing that you have the nerve to try to write at all.

Yes, indeed, most writers are really the meekest, most humble of human beings. It's hard to escape being just that way, at least till you have an enormous success. Rejections and criticisms are slapped at you from all directions, year after year.

But in another, deeper way, a writer has to be the greatest of all egoists and keep himself that way.

This is because in order to write at all you must feel that within *you*, in *your* emotions, mind, attitude, understanding of humanity, there is something different and special, worth being given immortality by the process of expression and the printed word. You must have a sort of sublime conceit, to believe that life does not owe you much of anything, but that you owe life, present and future, the wisdom and gems of your interpretation of that life process.

To keep this odd vanity breathing is one of a writer's greatest and toughest obligations to himself.

Let me tell you about my beginning writer friend. She wrote a story and bravely sent it to the *Saturday Evening Post*. She got it back with just one scribbled comment on it. "Too verbose." She sat down and cleaned out as many extra phrases as she could see. She put it in the mail.

She got it back again. This time the scribble said, "Somewhat better, but not right." She studied and tried to figure out what the scribbler meant and went to work. Mailed. Returned. "Flesh out your people a little. Revise end paragraph," it said this time.

You see the pattern, don't you? The upshot of the whole terrible time was that the scribbler at the *Post* began to get more interested with each rewrite and offered more comment. On the *ninth* try the *Post* bought the story. My friend was toasted by all the people who think writing is just a matter of words.

By the ninth try she was also not a beginning writer any longer. She was an accomplished one who had learned as she went along, by having faith in herself. By keeping that faith alive—and by keeping at it.

DON'T LET THEM GET TO YOU

Keep at it long enough, and you'll acquire a trait that has nothing to do with word-dexterity. In fact, you'll surely be sunk without it.

You must be stubborn. You have to be "stick-to-itive." You may reach a time of crisis when you want to quit. You long to. You have every reason to. But you don't.

One time during the Second World War, I worked on a newspaper all day and tried to write at night. I was new to writing, having sold only one story. Dog-tired most of the time, scrabbling for ideas, already mentally exhausted from a job as police reporter on a big newspaper in a vice-ridden wartime city, I kept batting them out in the evening.

I came home one night and there was a manila envelope from my new agent. In it was my latest hopeful story, and a letter saying kindly, but very firmly, that it smelled too much to taint the offices of any magazine. In it, also, were fourteen rejection slips.

I spread the whole mess out on the floor and stared at it through hot tears for a long time. I was through. Licked. Beaten. Done. Finished. I not only had to quit. I wanted to. Even if I was bawling my eyes out about it.

One hot bath, good dinner, cup of coffee, night's sleep later I started a new story. I'm glad I did.

STAYING ON TRACK

Words have little to do with the way a writer has to keep part of his mind to himself. Your mind goes perking along, carefully nurtured and trained to surmount almost any difficulties. No author in the world, most likely, has managed to write for long without having his personal life ruffled, upset, or even shot to pieces. All while he forced himself to make the small creatures on paper more real than the wife who left him, or the kids who were ill, or his own headache, the relatives who needed him, or the bills that plagued him. (Or *her*. Women authors' lives are further complicated by the responsibilities of a household and the nurturing that traditionally goes with the territory. Virginia Woolf's Angel in the House is right there, peering over the woman writer's shoulder, urging her to make the beds, chase the dustballs, cook a roast, pick up the kids, and deal with all crises, major and minor, along the way.)

No matter what your sex or age, you must hold tight to this second world—not the inner world of yourself exactly—but the secretly planned orbit of the piece of work you're doing. So, you rush home from a picnic or you wake up in the night or you grow suddenly silent in the midst of general conversation, and you find yourself *away* from the present moment as surely as if you stepped into a weird time machine.

Most of the time it's a good place to live, with those creatures of your creation. Of course, it's always a good idea to put your whole mind on whatever you do. But the *concentration* which allows you all of the leeway that real life doesn't have—where you can make people exactly what you want them to be, have them do whatever you want them to do in a world you control—can be rewarding and exhilarating to the spirit.

There is that other, more practical kind of concentration, too. The kind that shuts off the barking dog, the too-loud TV, the washer's hum, the tough workday behind you. You must concentrate a paragraph ahead, hold tight to the next chapter's plot, remember (in nonfiction) the words and inflection and expression of a person interviewed. A tape listened to. A verse to be included. A logical progression.

Without this ability to shut out the real and noisome world for the world of the mind, of make believe, writers just aren't worth their salt.

STOP, LOOK, AND LISTEN

A writer has to be an observer, too. If you've ever taken a walk with a photographer, you'll know how it is.

The very fact of the camera in his hand, loaded and ready, makes you look around for pictures. Trees, clouds, brooks, small flowers jump out at you with intensity, with framed composition, with clarity, as they never do when you're hurrying along the street toward an assigned destination.

To write is to avoid assigned destinations in a way. It is the walk for the walk's sake, a ramble, to taste the air, see the changing sky, watch the faces. It is to hold always within you as much wonder at what you see as if you were an adult child, kicking up dust and picking clover on a summer day. The child, or the photographer, or you, comes home from such a walk with something added to the person who began it. Joy for the child. Pictures for the photographer. And something to put into words for you.

That's the way it is with writers. If you don't see how it is yourself, you certainly aren't able to make other people see it. If you don't feel it yourself, how are you going to make other people feel anything?

LEARN TO LIVE WITH TENSION

Something that has no connection with your typewriter but which is a vital part of any writer is the ability to deal with tension as high as the most powerful wires. Four ways you get it, each of them rough.

First there is the dream, the search, the hunt, and the prayer for a germ of an idea, blown to you like a dust mote from some unexpected, eagerly anticipated source. A long wait, sometimes, and a hard one. But with waiting, with looking around, with allowing your inner self to simmer slowly, you will finally get an idea.

With it comes a momentary release from tension. You lie awake, feeling good, as if you had money in the bank because at last, at last, there is an idea in the kitty.

This is immediately replaced by more tension. There are those white, white sheets of blank paper to fill. You try to transfer that idea to paper, to phrases that will in some small way at least, present a little of the fine picture in your mind. This picture never comes whole. Never. No matter how long you write, the picture in the mind is always more beautiful, more touching, warm, and real than human limitations can make it.

But you clothe the skeletal idea and eventually it does get done. A certain joy hits you when the last sheet is yanked from the roller and the little pencil marks have had their field day and a nice clean copy is ready. You feel good. Limp, relaxed, cleansed, ready to laugh and celebrate.

For a couple of days you do.

Then it's time for the third nervousness. This is an unpleasant one. It's based on the simple fact that you have turned your priceless prose in to a professor. Or, if you're writing at a more advanced level, trying to sell, it has reached some editor somewhere. It is no longer your private property. It is about to be shared, commented on, thought about.

So now, the fourth and final phase. There's nothing comparable to hearing that first reaction—the heavy criticism which really hurts, or its happy alternative, a treasured handful of complimentary words. For the professional, a way of life depends on the answer. Either he's going to have to stall the phone company or he's going to be able to pay his income tax and maybe get a new pair of shoes if there's that much left over. There are, of course, some writers so well-heeled they don't know such problems. But they are strictly in the luxurious minority and they probably knew the problems once upon a time.

These, then, are the tools with which a writer works—tools far stronger and yet far finer, too, than any words in any dictionary. They are intangibles, much much more than phrases you can read back in black and white. They are, instead, the inspiration and the impetus that propel a writer forward into a larger, deeper area, a wider vision, a separate world.

So, realize before you ever begin to write that there is much more to it than the words which show on the page. Just as there is much more to you than the pleasantries you exchange with acquaintances at the post office, your classes, or at parties. Three quarters of the art of writing, and three quarters of you, like an iceberg, lie beneath the surface.

To find those hidden depths you must hold true to sensitivity and universality. You must have faith in the importance of writing and in yourself. You must be stubborn, able to deal with tension, patient, and must train your mind to live in your secret world, no matter what happens out of it. You must learn to observe, to see all things clearly and as completely as you can.

If you think like this consistently, even for a little while at a time, you're beginning to be a writer before you ever write a word.

Assignment

(Note: These assignments can be done effectively in class as each subject is discussed, or they can be done alone, one at a time or several examples of each, as your memory becomes alive and sharper.)

1. Write five sentences about a time when you felt that you were really sensitive to another human being or situation.

2. Write five sentences about a moment when you experienced a feeling of universality, a oneness with all people.

3. Write five sentences about a time when you either lost or found faith in yourself.

4. Write five sentences about a time when it paid you to be stubborn.

5. Write five sentences on why it is hard for you to concentrate and what distracts you.

6. Look out of the window and write five sentences about what you observe.

7. Write five sentences about tension and what makes you feel that way.

8. Write five sentences about why you are reading this book, or chose this class in the first place.

When this assignment is complete you will have taken the first step in the underlying meaning of writing itself. You will have put into words eight things about yourself that you have never before expressed on paper.

Now here is something to think about. You have really written something, right? What are you going to do with it?

Well, first of all and seriously, keep it!

This rule applies to everything you write. You're not always going to be at the stage you are now, you know. You're adding knowledge to knowledge, piece to piece. You're adding not only *words* but feelings, emotions, dreams, and talents to the vocabulary of your writing. You never know when they'll serve you.

I have a very well-known writer friend, who has been at it for many years, and has a closet (well, a couple of cartons) full of just such fragments as your five sentences. Time and again over the years, he tells me, he has searched through them for some nugget of gold he'd written in a rejected tale, or jotted down just as you have now.

There is really no bad story or article that doesn't have a gem of a sentence or two. Don't lose it.

Another advantage of keeping all your assignments is that later on, when you read about how to cut or change or rewrite or revise a piece of work, you can go back to your beginning. Believe me, it will hearten you to take some of your initial work and change it for the better.

Just as there is a set of intangibles that will work for you as you become a writer, so is there a counterlist which will work against you. Hazards, hurdles, brick walls—it doesn't matter what you call them. What counts, what is always most important (not only in writing but in all phases of endeavor, and even in living itself), is your attitude toward the things that can defeat you if you allow them to.

So, in logical fashion, your attitude toward this second list, which we can call "negative intangibles" and has little or nothing to do with words on paper, will make you a real writer or leave you an amateur, or a dropout. They are pointed out because just as it isn't fair to send a "green soldier" into battle, so is it unwise to rampage into the field of writing without knowing what or who your enemies are.

ENEMY AGENTS

Rejection and criticisms are one of the biggest hazards. From them, like the limbs from a tree, stem many other qualities. Some you must learn to fight and some you must acquire and treasure.

CHAPTER 2

It's Up To You

A piece of writing—a story, article, poem, essay, any kind of writing from high school to polished professional, is like your baby. He may be homely compared to some, but you have conceived him and carried him and finally, in pain, managed to get him breathing and seeing the light of day.

It's not easy to have somebody say of your earthly child, "My, he's an ugly little tyke, isn't he?"

It's not an easy thing to have a rejection slip say "too autobiographical," "slight plot," "too slick," "not quite right for us at this time." Or a professor, under that unhappy D, write, "Your ideas are scattered, diffused, disorganized, usual, and you have expressed them in as confused a manner as possible."

It doesn't help either, that such remarks come from someone you consider a good friend—the professor or the editor who the last time around thought you were great and well on your way. This piece of writing, the one they despise and tell you so clearly, is, after all, your youngest child and doubly precious for his newness, his helplessness.

DUST YOURSELF OFF
Many a new writer has fallen flat on his face never to rise again because his belief in his ability was no larger than the comments that turned down his effort. Many a new writer, conversely, has stayed a new one and an unpublished one because he rushed too wildly to the defense of his child and refused to acknowledge that, being his, it could be less than perfect.

Criticism and rejection slips, like the poor, are always with us. For the selling writer some of them will be machine printed, cold, and indifferent. Some will have a scribble on them, like my friend of the nine tries. Some will be a sentence or two. And as you work and sell, occasionally there will be those from editors who know you, are truly sorry they can't use the piece, and will be kind enough to ask to see other work. Or, in school, there will be teachers who nourish your spark even as they find fault with it, and thus help you to try again and to improve.

COPING WITH "MISS BUT"

Some rejections can make you tear your hair. I snatched myself almost bald for years with one editor (who actually bought quite a few things and must then be taken seriously) whom I called "Miss But"!

The first paragraph of all of her letters was warm and admiring. Her comments might run something like this:

> " 'Too Early in the Morning,' is one of the most charming ideas I've run across in a long, long time. It has a human touch, a moving and exciting plot, characters who move and have their being in a real-to-life setting."

Soaking up a paragraph like that I would begin to purr while I was still näive, and read on eagerly.

> "*But,*" the letter inevitably went on, "it falls apart in the middle, nobody is interested in that kind of background, our readers couldn't identify with that sort of people, and the whole thing wanders and doesn't seem to get anywhere. I am so very sorry."

Well, I was, too! And I was also afraid that I didn't have what it took, could never write another story, was in the wrong business anyhow—at the precise time that I was also burning up with anger at the stupidity of the rejecter's thinking.

Of course, some rejections are reasonable. Editors always have an inventory and perhaps your ideas parallel one they've already bought. Perhaps it wasn't right for them anyhow, and another market would be better.

So we must find that happy medium which retains our faith in our potential and keeps us working, at the same time admit that there is still much to learn. And a great deal of that learning can be from those rejections, those remarks, those grades.

It's up to you, and that is the beginning of *attitude*.

What choice do you have?

You can read over those pieces which have failed, brood over them, mourn if you will, and give up, saying, "I've shot my wad. I've given my all. I'm just no good. Whatever made me think I had what it takes to be a writer?"

You can storm, "Those teachers! Those editors! They don't know a good story when it hits them over the head."

Or you can settle down with your work, read it over and see where it's weak. Yes, you can.

Oh, it isn't easy. Any more than it would be simple to admit that your nose was too long, your hair too mousy, your stomach too big. Criticism is a double-edged knife, hard to nick yourself, harder to have pointed at you by someone else. But you can learn to criticize yourself if you concentrate on what you want to be as a writer.

JUST FORGET IT—FOR NOW

First, you put it away. It's a finished work. It didn't make its way those first times out. But it is part of you and can be improved. Someday. After a while.

Set your mind on your next project and work all the way through to the end of that. Then, come some rainy day when you're at loose ends, you pull out the rejected manuscript, settle down with a cup of coffee or tea, put your feet up, and do a strange but possible thing.

Remember reading back there about leading two lives? The external and the internal and how the search here is for the internal? Well, now, you sort of reverse the process. You try to get out of your own writing (the inner) personality and put your external "mask" back on, (not for long!) and back into the shape of your own skin.

Maybe you can help this process along by reading a story in a magazine by somebody else, like putting on reading glasses after using distance ones. Try to see in that story the weaknesses, the flaws, the errors large or small.

Then, with your mind still impersonal, switch to your own work. Read it slowly. Try to forget the effort you put into it, the special phrases you "just adored."

In real life, when you bury your ego and think of the welfare of those around you—especially those who are your nearest and dearest—your horizon opens and your self narrows. Sometimes when you look at a sunset, or a new moon, or a child's upturned face, you forget yourself entirely.

If you can do it in real life, you can do it with the thoughts, people, and actions you have set on paper. But like all worthwhile things, it takes time and patience to acquire.

I promise you though, if you'll pretend till it seems real to be somebody else—a reader and nothing else—you'll be able to note the exact point where you lost interest or wandered off on a tangent or expressed yourself badly.

Try it.

As you work along, trying not to fear those enemies of rejection and criticism, you find out that the teachers and the editors—most of them—know whereof they speak. Editors know their readers. They choose for them. They have seen thousands of manuscripts over the years.

Professors, who have read hundreds of books of all kinds, who perhaps have written themselves, who have slaved to be at least fairly expert in their area, know more than you about writing—and can only show you the way by telling you where you are wrong as well as right.

So you admit it. Maybe your youngest was a little skinny, but you find that you can either put a little healthy flesh on him or you can have another brain child who may be perfect and full of vitality.

By the time you've managed this sort of working and thinking, all fear and hurt have dissipated and you're left with just the residue of normal disappointment because you didn't make it the first time.

SMALL, MEDIUM, OR LARGE?

This is the way it is. The world is filled with writers who never get a word published. Or just an occasional word. They work hard. They write well—some of them. But they never see the light of print.

This is because of their egos. Ego here has a very different meaning from the strong, good one which will make you feel that you have something of yourself to share with the world. This type of ego will not compromise. Each word is diamond-studded. Each idea is superior. Each subject is deeper and different from any other. If they aren't understood, it's because the whole of modern civilization is stupid. Everybody else is out of step.

This kind of ego is stubborn, too. But it's the kind of mulishness that will keep these writers from going anywhere. They also have faith—but in the false god of vanity. These people are writing to *be* writers. Or to say they are writers. Or to run around in odd attire, pretending they are writers. You see them in droves at certain types of writers' club meetings or in the dark little cafes. They are writing to please themselves, writing to express themselves as obscurely as possible. It's all right for false prestige or therapy. But they never get a word published.

These people have strange and complex egos which lead to an attitude of self-sufficiency, which in turn leads to a viewpoint which is quite opposite to the feeling of universality which is so important to writers. They think they are sharing their deepest and wisest thoughts, and so they are. But too often these thoughts are only for their own enjoyment and are apt to lose the sense of identification with the wider world. They are so absorbed in their own personalities that they have trouble communicating with those around them. It's a narcissistic form of writing.

For many years now, off and on, I have taught creative writing, in Rochester, New York, in southern California, and on the eastern shore of Maryland. Each class has had more than its share of talent, whether it was for children or for adults of all ages.

Each class in the adult area, however, was also loaded with more than its share of the ego-writer. They had one great thing in common.

They concentrated on tragedy. All was significant. All was symbolic. All was downbeat. All was troubled and angry, with no solution to anything. Tragedy for tragedy's sake. And all was mighty depressing to read. And totally unsalable.

Yet all of those students had experiences within the realm of their own lives, their own observations, which would have made fine, warm, vital stories, articles or poems. They didn't see them. They thought about people they'd never met, wrote about places they'd never seen. Everything turned out to be a pair of lovers jumping off the cliff because life was so grim, grueling, appalling, and meaningless.

They also thought that they'd be proven great. Someday. Some far day, they and their precious words would be appreciated.

It's easy to let this sort of thinking sneak into your daily life. Writing is hard work. When your friend, to whom you shyly read a few paragraphs, looks at you and says, "I don't get it," it's very simple to rationalize, "Well, he's not so smart after all."

When the criticism comes, it's no chore to ease the hurt by saying, "I'm ahead of my time. I'm too good for them."

Continued, this kind of rationalization becomes part of you (as it has with many talents in all of the creative arts) and you diminish yourself, your ability, and your present work by thinking of yourself as a someday-great!

Incidentally and just in passing, this sort of thinking can get to be a habit in every area, so that you excuse any and all failures with the fact that other people just don't understand. Dangerous!

When the enemy of this ego approaches, ask yourself a question.

"How can any writer be certain he or she will interest the future and far-flung generations, if he or she can't communicate, can't give something—right now? This moment? To contemporaries? In the modern media—newspaper, television, magazines and books? Today?"

Remind yourself of something, too. Maugham, Steinbeck, Hemingway, Welty, Faulkner, O'Connor, Saroyan, Parker, Salinger, Mailer—all of them and dozens of others wrote for the popular media, fitted themselves into short story and serial patterns and learned their craft by that fitting. Further back, Dickens, Twain, O. Henry, Stevenson—all of that happy crew practically wrote on order. If there had been such media in Shakespeare's time there is more than an off-chance that his plays would have been serialized before they were produced. Even so, he wrote prolifically for entertainment of those regular, average people of his era.

In short, beat off the dragon of ego-bad by realizing that those writers wrote for their neighbors, for the people around them, friends and enemies. They wrote to be understood.

When I was writing short stories constantly, I never finished a first draft but I took it into my mother's room. She lived with us, wasn't well, and thoroughly enjoyed those times when I "read to her." If there was one thing, large or small, that my mother didn't understand instantly and fully in any of those stories—out it came before the finished version. Always. My mother was the average, fairly intelligent, simple and honest person for whom I was writing and I knew that if she appreciated and comprehended the story, the readers would very likely do the same.

CONDESCENDING TO SPEAK

Ego-bad leads logically to condescension. Once an intellectual young writer looked down his nose at my whole writing life.

"Magazines!" he cried scornfully. "I'd rather be dead."

Everybody writes within a circle. If that young man wants to write in the circle of the obscure, the remote, the ego we've just discussed, let him. It's not our circle here.

Anyone will go along with the would-be greats up to the point of admitting that today's markets—stage, TV, movies, magazines or books—are not always of high literary quality. Some of them are desperately inferior.

But the writer—beginning or assured—should not ever feel a sense of condescension toward those markets. They are the stuff of the modern world, and to condescend is to deny that world. It is the same as looking down on your next-door neighbor, the man around the corner, people of another race, a cowboy, a recording artist, a clubwoman, a rioter, a vegetarian, a roommate, a Bircher, a soldier, a teacher, a housewife. These are real people with real problems solved with courage and dignity, one way or the other. They are your material. You live with them and their problems.

This young intellectual's arrogant way of looking at the commercial part of the writing world is an ever-present threat to the beginning writer. If you can't sell your work there are magazines that will publish it for nothing and give you copies as payment. This leaves you feeling, among your family and friends, at least, like the real thing. But the work is really not deeper or greater because it is "literary."

There are vanity publishing houses who will turn your longer efforts into good-looking hardbound books. You fork out the money. They publish a certain number of copies and retain a high percentage of any books sold. The local bookstore will stock them as a favor if they know you. You are right in there among the authors who fought to get published the hard way.

Go the route of the young man, but do not look down on the "slicks" or even the "pulps." There's nothing wrong with working to be paid for your work. Honestly, there isn't. Nor about having it published where millions of people can find it, share it, understand it, and perhaps gain something from it.

A warning here. Because you manage to get paid doesn't mean that you can sit down and write just for money, though. The sight of the long green—or rather, your desire for it—always shows through. You have to write because you want to say something; again, just as well as you can.

Somehow editors, who have spent so much of their lives staring at various writings, seem to know by page three that you are not sending out the message, "I have something beautiful and fresh to share." They know very quickly that you're begging, "I'm hungry. Please feed me."

You do not have to be a new writer to make this error. Ernest Hemingway, who wrote the exquisite *Old Man and the Sea*, proved it beyond any doubt when he wrote *Across the River and Into the Trees*.

Garbled, mixed in thought and metaphor, filled with obscenities (at least for that day), only his name could have gotten it published. And he lost followers right and left with its appearance.

So, please, wait until you have something to say. Don't try to write it because you want a word processor.

Humility is an invaluable asset for keeping you on the right track. It proves itself again and again as a good friend whose head never swells no matter how famous you get. With pride in check you won't try to write for money alone. Nor will you aim for future generations only.

MORE SNAKES IN THE GARDEN

There are other things which threaten a good attitude toward the writing craft. They are outside things which, on the face of it, you can't do much about. There aren't as many general markets today as there once were. Many established writers are having a tough go of it. You will find people trying to dissuade you from this area of creativity and interest.

Pay no attention to them. Remember that you are *you*. You are fresh and new with things to be said in a way they have never been said before. Competition is a lion you need never face. Consider him old and toothless because he has lived forever. Start your journey with a light heart. Don't weigh yourself down with the enemies of fear of criticism, rejection, extreme egotism, or condescension.

A wise agent said to me a long time ago, "It is my job to show you how to write things that editors will want to buy. It is not my job to go around trying to change the editors' minds about what they *want* to buy."

This is the attitude you need. This is the way you start fitting together a jigsaw puzzle of many colors and shapes, making a coherent whole that will have beauty of expression, simplicity of emotion, reality of characters, movement of plot, and newness of thought. And which will extend outward to the world from you—from what you are. As you discover your hidden self, you begin to *write* inside-out.

So now you are ready to start. The stage before the beginning is over. You can pull a sheet of paper toward you and sharpen that pencil you've been holding all this time.

Assignment

1. Read a few pages of a novel or short story or article. Pretend you are a writing teacher and criticize it (for good or bad) in three sentences.

2. Express in three sentences, the type of writing that most interests you.

3. Make a list of your recent reading that held your attention more than most and in each case tell why in one sentence.

4. Make a list of the reasons why you enjoy writing.

Go back over this assignment, and look for the elements we've discussed so far. For instance:

1. In what ways does the author show sensitivity, universality, faith, stubbornness—all of the intangibles we've discussed.

2. Find a book or a short story or article that embodies the kind of writing you'd like to do.

3. In the reading you preferred, identify every point of value that you think we have made so far.

4. No assignment—just hope you have a good reason.

CHAPTER 3

*Know
Yourself*

How wonderful it would be if, from the very start, a writer could sit down and set a story, full-blown, perfectly formed and sharply plotted, on paper! You know, as if he had absorbed the whole technique by a sort of osmosis and the act of living.

Sadly, except in very special and rare cases, this is not so.

It has happened that the first story of an untrained writer, put together by instinct, and because the story itself was dreamed of for a long time, has been successful.

I have in mind a complete-in-one-issue novel, published in the same issue of a magazine in which my first little short story managed to make its way. There was a great to-do about this author. I envied her the good long story, the fact that the movies bought it, and that her name was immediately well known. She was set up and established with her first effort and that is always wonderful.

There was also the time when my husband started to play golf. Well-coordinated, naturally athletic and with a large handicap, within six weeks he won the club tournament.

You may remember the glorious voice, "the greatest since Caruso" everybody said, which burst upon the world a generation ago, pure, untrained, a miracle.

All three cases started out with a bang, at the top, so to speak.

But the writer who had such excitement over her first story was never heard from again, except that she got some sort of job in the story department of a movie studio.

The singer, lured by the offers of enormous sums of money in the entertainment field, never took a lesson—and, tragically, sang himself out with that unsupported voice which was too big for him to use and protect without training.

My husband, on the crest of his championship, began to take lessons to learn how to do it *right*. For years his score stayed right up there with the duffers.

Of the three my husband was, and is, the only real winner. Realizing that his first success was a "fluke," he has learned golf as it should be played, from the very basics, and has been a consistently good performer for a long time. Because he knew what he was doing, he had something to depend on every time he picked up a club.

This approach is particularly important for those who want to write. It's hard to be patient because we're dealing with words. Not a paintbrush awkward in our hands. Or piano keys on which our fingers stumble because we're unfamiliar with them. We have always used words. Most stories or any other kind of writing in general, seem simple to read. It's hard to hold back, to learn a little at a time.

But if you don't want to be a one-shot writer—if you want to continue working and advance year after year—you study your craft in small doses till you know what you're doing in every phase of it.

Yes, I sold my first story. I didn't know much about how to write a short story at the time. But I *did* know how to write. I had four years of newspaper work and six years of writing for radio behind me before I attempted even three consecutive pages of a story.

THE WRITE STUFF

Writing, and learning to write, *is* that jigsaw puzzle mentioned earlier. You have to become proficient in dibs and dabs. You learn one little thing at a time, practice it, become good at it, and then you go on to the next thing. Enough of this sort of working theory, and the dibs and dabs can be fitted neatly, sometimes excitingly, together.

And you know what you're doing in every area!

Of all the myriad troubles, minor and major, which assail any of us who want to write, getting started is the highest hurdle. It doesn't in the least matter whether you've written for a quarter of a century or for five minutes. To know *where* to begin is a treasured individual secret in the separate minds of both those unknown and those famous.

This applies tightly to *where* to begin to *learn* to write.

When you learn to write from the *inside-out*, you have a place to start.

You start with yourself.

I REMEMBER MAMA

Writers often proudly say, "I have total recall!"

They say it the way a good musician points out that he has perfect pitch. A great many of them, musicians and writers, do possess the thing they brag about. Instinctively.

More often, though, total recall is buried under the thousand acts of daily living. In that case it has to be cultivated. It has to be coaxed and worked on until it begins to be part of your conscious thinking.

And it can be. On demand. It must be, because without it, and without being able to think and write on demand, you're a lost author.

What is total recall?

Literally translated it means "remembering everything," doesn't it? That's just what it is.

You sit there where you are, with that clipboard and pencil. You begin to train yourself in this most vital and necessary action. You can't write off the top of your mind, the rim of your heart. You must dig deep and pull long to make whatever you *do* write a piece that is uniquely your own.

But you don't use the pencil just yet. Before you can *write* on demand you have to learn to *think* on demand.

First of all, prepare yourself for it. Different people find recall in different ways. You don't necessarily have to be alone—some of you may be in a classroom instead of at home. But you do have to gear yourself to shut off the noisome world. As some do with meditation. You sort of pull into yourself for a little while.

Others require absolute quiet, and find a corner where there is no distraction, no chance of being interrupted. For some, it's almost like going into a dream, so they lie down comfortably—on a bed, back in a chair, at a quiet beach.

And it can be learned, so that you attempt to find your past whenever you need to. Over and over. And you make that backward search for as long as you feel comfortable with it.

Let's try an experiment, a thought-exercise. No writing. Here is our first step.

1. Close your eyes, be quiet. Dream a little. Let your mind wander back to this time last year. Don't force it. Don't hurry. You'll hit a nugget, a piece of gold, something that has stayed with you for a whole twelve months.

2. Once you have found it, polish it a little. Try to recall the atmosphere that surrounded it, the background, the people who were there, and note carefully the expressions on their faces, the things they said. But above all, remember how they affected you, how you *felt*.

3. Now, let's take it a little further. Try to remember how it was when you were fourteen or so. You don't have to be that exact age. Just move back in time to when you first felt practically adult and ready to face the world.

I wish we were sitting together in the same room, that I could be with you as you tell what you thought and that I could share my remembering with you.

1. I saw this little house where I'm working now, as it was last year, a worn, torn, beat-up old place, waiting for our paint and effort. I felt the pleasure of the work it took to make something charming from so very little—a sanctuary for two high-pressured people.

2. I walked into a new high school and found a long-lipped, dour principal and could see his crossed feet beneath his desk, and could feel my heart race as I tried to get the courage to make this change into a strange world.

There's a still longer journey for which you're partially prepared by your memories so far.

3. Reach way back. Go ahead; don't worry about it. Reach into your childhood, anywhere in it, and pick out a sort of plum. Remember Mama. Remember Grandmother. Remember that mean teacher in the third grade or the first day of school, or the time you swiped something from the dime store. Or further yet, yourself as a tiny child before a hearth perhaps, trying to maneuver one sock.

Come on back now. You don't want to stay there. You have one more place to go. This is your last attempt. This is the real stretching. It's much harder for adults, so far from it, than for children.

4. Try to reach all the way back to the first thing you remember. Your first conscious impression. Don't get mixed up with stories you were told about your babyhood. Find it yourself, that new-old day of impressions which had no words because you had no words.

Let me give you an example. It's from a very long book I've been working on for years—sadly unpublished, and more sadly, unfinished. But it starts with a section called "The Lost Years"—and that is all total recall.

At first it was just a matter of feeling. Her cheek leaned against mine. Because it was as round as my own there was only one small circle of contact, like two fat people bumping bellies at the moment of love.

She set her arms around me, too, one tense and tight against my back, squeezing my shoulder blades together, the other jamming the sides of my knee bones. All the front of me was concentrated and warmed by the pillow softness of her breasts. I forgot the points of discomfort as she moved her shoulders from side to side in delicious friction. My grandmother was starch and Cuticura soap. My mother was bones and uncertainty. My father was muscle and scraping beard. My grandfather was bristle and acrid. No one else had touched me. This lush depth, the feeling of sinking into something immeasurable, was like sleep. I dug closer.

She pushed me away suddenly, letting go in all areas except my knees. It brought her face, enlarged, a few inches from mine. She wore a trimmed hat and there were many small bright flowers on it. I sniffed for them, but the sweetness was not there. It was on her breath which came at me in rapid puffs, each one laden, as if she were filled with an inner perfume which sprayed me and would remain when she was gone.

My mother was in the room somewhere, she must have been, but I do not remember her presence. There was no world except those arms and breasts and breath, and that face.

She walked with me to the window. I was aware of dazzle and sun upon my back, at the identical moment the golden touch came upon her face.

She said, in a kind of voice I had never heard, low, cracked, turned in upon itself, "Baby Judy, as long as you live, never, never do anything that will make you ashamed to stand in God's sunshine!"

I stared at her lips, red as a cherry on the outside, showing pale vulnerable pink as they moved against her white teeth. Something about the pinkness embarrassed me so that I went quickly to her eyes.

They seemed to be lakes, worlds, wholes of something. The circles were outlined in deep blue and filled with a thousand shades, the gold of the sun caught, splattered, alternating in no pattern, like aggies floating in cream, in the whites untouched by age, pure as a child's, no red lines anywhere. The black lashes top and bottom were fences protecting this purity, this magic.

I looked from one to the other, taking each alone, absorbed in the duplication and the strange drowning. From the cliff of the lower lids, creeping suicidally, two silver tears moved outward, clung reluctant and afraid, then threw themselves over the edge. They missed the undershelf of the sockets, landing on the round cheeks. I watched them disintegrate and cut paths, thin and straggling, through the pink rouge and powder. When they thinned out against the corners of her mouth, I began to yell.

This is what I came up with. If *you* really tried, wasn't it sort of interesting, maybe even exciting? Your whole life has gone by you. There is more to you than you realized. There you are, grown up and a little tired, reading a little book about writing or talking about it in class, wondering whether or not you can write at all. Or can write more. Or can write better. You *are* going to write. You have a place to start any time you want to.

What's more, you've begun to accept a very tough and necessary form of discipline. You've made yourself *think* on demand. You haven't permitted yourself the alibi, "I can't think of anything," which can be a rearing wall between you and your work any day of the year.

GETTING IN GEAR

By beginning to cultivate total recall, you are taking the first steps that will help you get words together on paper. What you've done here is to reach backward and inward. Always, in all people, if sincerely tried, it brings forth something worth discovering and remembering. Above all, something worth writing down.

You can do it when you're putting yourself to sleep. Remember houses you've lived in. Remember how you felt and what you were like when you lived there. Remember passing faces of people you knew, relatives you loved. Remember anything and everything that will move your mind backward with the nostalgia which could create a mood for writing about other times, other places, and your other, younger self.

When you have practiced and remembered, long and hard, you begin to write it. You do it in any haphazard fashion you wish. Jot down whatever comes to you. Ignore punctuation and paragraphing. Just get it down.

This may seem vague or silly to you now. But it's an important piece of the jigsaw and fits with many other pieces. It has a practical application to the act of creative writing. It is the way to get started.

And it's more. It is the beginning of the mental discipline which will force you to think on demand and will eventually enable you to write on demand. It's the method that will transport you to various places, into the minds of people of various ages, so that you can extend your range of characters and events.

If you take those steps, those explorations into your own past—if you set them down as fully and richly as you humanly can—in as simple straightforward words as you can find—you will be a writer. Not a published writer, or one who knows how to put a story together or plot a novel. Nothing comes full-blown, remember.

But you will be a writer, nonetheless. You'll be expressing a brand new viewpoint—your own! You'll be remembering old experiences in a new way. You'll express them in a new combination of phrases—your own!

You'll also know how to open a door. You know that when you want to write a story set last year, courtship, high school, childhood, or first dreams, you have a place to go to find the emotions and the setting. A door backward. Into yourself. You'll discover it's a fascinating place. Even if you never write a word.

Assignment

1. Write five sentences about the first day on a new job.

2. Write five sentences about a high school experience that you sharply recall.

3. Write five sentences about the first trip you took as a child.

4. Write, at any length you can manage, the earliest experience you remember.

These exercises can be continuous, dependent on whatever flashes in your mind. They can be something you put together just for fun, or for remembering yourself, or for future generations of yours to read so that they may know you better.

You can, of course, try to search them out chronologically if you like, so that you have a consistent piece of work. But you're more apt to get them in varying flashes. And they should be written down in as complete form as possible, each time they occur to you.

Suggested Reading
First few chapters of *Swann's Way*, by Marcel Proust.
First few chapters of *Jean Christophe*, by Romain Rolland.

CHAPTER 4

Digging Deeper

In beginning to write you don't have to stay in the past, of course. It's important that you don't. You must not be stuck in the "good old days" any more than the older folks should live there.

So you try to write something new, something to add to your total recall and take you still another step ahead.

LIFE IS BUT A STREAM (OF CONSCIOUSNESS)

When I first discovered stream of consciousness I almost drowned in it for awhile. Every class I've ever taught—once it catches on—has done just about the same and was reluctant to go on to other techniques. Stream is fun. It's therapy. It's pure letting go.

What is stream of consciousness?

It's just writing, as fast as you can, everything—but *everything*—that passes through your mind during a given time. You let the subconscious mind do this for you. Don't stretch to say something that seems to sound good, or that is smart or wise, or for anybody else to read. Just write, not even worrying about making sentences, letting your phrases be broken and small. You just let out the drift and flow that is inside you.

You see, this stream of consciousness (or subconscious) never stops for a single fractional second. It goes rolling along like Ol' Man River. Sometimes it's on its own. Sometimes it's combined with planned thinking. It's never easily secured because its movement is rapid and rippling. But any writer has to try to catch it if he ever wants one single character to come alive. Many great writers have brought it to a wide ocean.

Make a business of this if you really want to find your way to your characters, the people in your tales. Be consistent. Each day, or each evening before you retire, sit down at a table or desk with the paper and the sharp pencil in front of you. You sit and wait; you stare around. Finally—away you'll go, pencil flying like haunted automatic writing, word after word, all thoughts going too fast for the mechanics of your hand and the letters. On and on.

It's a butterfly net in your hand, flashing in the light of your mind, catching as many of those bright slippery thoughts as you can before they escape you.

You want to know what this has to do with making people come alive on paper?

To repeat: A writer has to know himself before he can know anyone else or make him breathe. At all levels he has to explore himself. His racing mind. His inner thoughts. His delights and frustrations. If he doesn't, he's not going to be able to understand the most simpleminded person created by his typewriter. Stream of consciousness accomplishes this purpose.

In a more practical way it accomplishes still more. It gives speed to writing itself. It shows the fingers how to follow the mercurial mind. It makes for flexibility. Above all, what the writer has been able to do with his own thoughts he can, in time, do with the thoughts of those about whom he writes. Thus, they live.

It's not always easy to get started on stream. Sometimes it seems the thoughts are too minute, too quick, too personal to be snagged. But relax once more. Sit there quietly. Look around if you like. Take a quick peek at some stream writing my preteen pupils did, just to get the idea.

> Wrote Dickie:
> I am looking at the flies on the floor and wondering what it would be like to be a fly. Crawling around looking at the filthy things on the floor. Looking at the air cooler I can feel the cool breezes flowing across my face, like swimming in a cool mountain stream, clinging to rocks and letting the water rush by me.
> Wrote Sandra:
> The grass is blazing. I see a meadow with lots of flowers blooming. There is a boy and girl sitting in

it. They're in love. The boy is telling her he is leaving for the war. She cries. He leaves and she kills
herself.

Wrote Hugh:

The lure of something unknown—vigilant
night—palace balcony—tapa cloth—sun on it—
shadows on grass—hell of deep green—dark forest
crossed with sun and leaves.

Wrote David:

Airport on fire. Men getting killed. Tractor
fighting fire falling in ditch with burning log in it.
Smoke billowing in air. Ink spilling. Fifth grade
shuffling feet. Trees swing in wind. Chair by Mr.
W's desk. Greg hitting me. Mrs. L being nice in
history.

So there you are.

Assignment

It's a good idea for the professor or teacher to tell the young writers
that what they write of stream won't be read aloud, nor shared with
anyone except that teacher. You never know what will come out in
this form of writing—in aggressions, bad language, personal fears
and frustrations. To keep it confidential is to keep it free. And for
those working alone? Hide your notebook!

1. Now for exactly five minutes try to capture a running flow of everything that goes through your mind. Ignore punctuation again
and grammar and above all, forget that someone may read it. This
will only inhibit you and make you censor your words as they come
out.

2. Every night for exactly five minutes write stream of consciousness in a notebook or on dated papers.

Suggested Reading

"Palimpsest" (long poem), by Conrad Aiken

I AM THE KIND OF PERSON WHO

Now, there is a further step in this self business, this trying to turn natural selfishness into an advantage. I discovered it quite by accident and it has stood me in good stead ever since.

One day, empty of ideas, a little forlorn about life itself, with a wonder in me as to what I was anyhow, I doodled on a piece of paper, "I am the kind of person who. . . ."

Would you believe it? I worked on that analysis of myself for three whole days off and on. I thoroughly enjoyed every minute of it. I would wake in the morning with another great "revelation" about the person who lived in my skin, and would race downstairs to put it into words before I forgot who I was!

I tried hard to be honest. Sometimes I succeeded, although I was always conscious of pulling a few punches just in case anybody found the busy sheets after I was dead.

This, incidentally, is an attitude that will haunt you in all writing. The fist yanks back just a little, afraid to hurt self or neighbor, friend or relative with too much truth. To be honest with yourself and your writing is one thing. To hurt good people with brutal frankness is quite another.

When I was finished, what I had written could have been turned over to a more professional writer, one who didn't know me at all. He would have been able to write a story about me, to make me walk, talk, have my being as large as life. Probably, just because he didn't know me personally, it would be more interesting than life, too.

It was good for me, this "I am the kind of person who." I got along with myself better from then on. It was a piece of work, like a large sprawling unfinished novel, which I could revise yearly, add to and subtract from. I would never be able to finish it until the last day of my life.

To give you an even clearer idea—here is the "I am the kind of person" one of my current students wrote:

> I am the sort of person who paves the road to hell
> with good intentions but doesn't get around to fol-
> lowing most of them through. When I hear of an
> occasion to write a quick note of sympathy, con-
> gratulation, hope you are better, I really plan to re-
> spond, but the days go by, and pretty soon the oc-

casion has changed or is so far in the past that it's no longer relevant. Procrastination is my sin. Maybe it will go away by tomorrow or next week, and it never does. I am continually being embarrassed by this weakness, but never to the point where I really reform. People who keep up to date in their correspondence are objects of my envy.

I'm neat only in spots. There are always areas that will not bear inspection. It pains me, but not enough. I'm always ready to leave the house to itself and go off on any pretext. Housework is so always with you. Nothing is really accomplished. Clothes promptly get dirty all over again, meals have to be prepared, eaten, cleaned up after and that routine repeated several times a day, day after day. A tidy, clean house becomes a dusty dirty house. Nothing is ever done so that you can look back and say that it will last for a while.

I love to be outdoors. The walks we took in the mornings last year were a great source of pleasure. Nothing can equal the feeling of being on your toes, physically, and I want it back.

I like happy people around me. Who doesn't? Children are fun most of the time. Every once in a while you get an insight into the workings of a young mind that is most rewarding.

I love springtime and, of late, think that I'm really going out and enjoy it. I may never see another. Once I sat under a blossoming apple tree in Maine as long as I wanted to and really looked at it, a rare opportunity.

I tend to worry about things that never happen, and will never learn to take it easy till there's something to worry about. Snap judgments are another of my weaknesses. To be proven wrong so many times should show me the folly of such. First impressions are not to be heavily relied upon. Some of my good friends didn't seem at all my type on first meeting.

I am the sort of person who drops things, knocks things over, creates general mayhem, forgets things, leaves things behind.

I think that I need lots of sleep, at least eight hours per, and I tend to look bedraggled and droopy if I don't get it, circles and sags.

I hate canning and preserving and everybody expects me to have stacks of jelly and jam. Mine are always syrup or else they develop a thin layer of mold.

People are always saying, "Let me do that," and grab. I want to do it. I'm tired of being treated like an idiot child, with a patronizing pat on the head.

I do a nice beef stew.

So it's your turn. Head up that paper and find out about yourself.

Assignment

Write "I am the kind of person who"—and begin to figure yourself out. This may be started in class but it should be continued from day to day. Maybe there will only be a phrase or a couple of sentences to add. But as you keep thinking about who you are and what makes you tick, you'll keep making new discoveries. Catch them all on paper.

These three then, these helpful three, are with you to stay. They are a trio of jigsaw pieces that fit neatly together and get you started. You can clearly see the journey of "learning to write" from your inner sources is on its way.

You've drawn some of your past out into the light with total recall.

You've expressed your constant flitting thoughts with stream of consciousness.

You've seen yourself through your own eyes in honest estimate, to bring yourself alive for others to see as a character with "I am the kind of person who."

Continue to do these three things. Do them until you feel fluent in each area. In time, when practicing approaches a sort of near-perfect, you will tie them all together in a story that has nothing to do with you really. But it will come *from* you in the true sense. In time you will add all the other jigsaw pieces and the continuity from inside to out will be clear. Right now, though, take the next step and find out how to move outward into a larger world.

CHAPTER 5

Where Do Characters Come From?

A renowned magazine editor told me once, and I think he said it to everybody who was new to writing, "The greatest plots are in our daily newspapers. We read them and usually forget them. That's because we don't know the people involved. They're not close enough for us to feel their suffering.

"So it doesn't matter if your plot is highly complicated or terribly dramatic. Nothing very great or overwhelming has to happen to your characters. What matters is that the reader *cares* what happens, no matter how little. That the character becomes real to him."

Some characters do leap right off the pages of the daily news, of course. A family in a strange town with no money. A child hurt or desperately ill. A man of great courage. When their experiences are read about the public swamps them with gifts, money, cards, letters.

Why do they?

For the same reason the magazine editor spoke of. A responsive chord struck in the heart, mind, or experience of the reader. Not necessarily the situation, tragic or drastic. More like the clear sharp idea of an average human striving, trying, bucking to get by, caught in troubles too big for him, fighting to survive them.

This is called *identification*.

To do any sort of positive, constructive, vital writing you must come to grips, first of all, with this word.

You must, first, identify with your characters.

You must, second, make your characters identify with the reader.

Or, reverse it if it makes it clearer to you. Make the reader identify with your characters. The result is the same.

This isn't quite as easy as it sounds. We'll soon explore it in depth. But for the moment, it can be reduced to a couple of sentences.

You know how it is. You have so much to do and you go about your business. Most of the time, despite your concern about the present state of the world, it's as if your eyes were tight shut and your ears closed to what's happening around you. Your own thoughts and feeling and events are absorbing and important.

That's fine and dandy for a normal, fairly selfish human being. It's zero for a writer.

WHO CARES?

So we try to find that chord which the sad news stories resonated in every character we write about. We try to make the reader *care*, as that editor explained.

One of the best ways to do this is with careful, well-planned *motivation*.

What is motivation?

It is, "that within the individual, rather than without, which incites him to action; any idea, need, emotion, or state that prompts to an action."

In other words, when you write anything about anybody (even about yourself) you try to figure out why he acts the way he does; what upsets him; what his background was and is; why he should be happy or unhappy; how he talks and reasons; what he likes and dislikes. (As you can see, both sensitivity and universality peek through.)

If you manage to do these almost miracle-working things on a piece of paper, you'll have a character who doesn't make a false move. He's always himself, with a good reason or a solid compulsion for everything he does, says, or feels. You have, in a way, "explained" him because *you* know him. If he comes totally alive to *you*, you are able to transmit what you know. Your reader will identify with him no matter how strange he may be.

Of course, that is entirely too great a concept for any beginner and even for a seasoned writer many times. But it must be worked toward and there are some concrete ways to do that.

You already started when you began to search for meaning within yourself by writing "I am the kind of person who." You looked for your *own* motivations in that process, trying to find out what makes you spring to action, just as you'll later do with every character you write about.

THE LIFE SOURCE

This is where characters begin to come from. Again from the inside of you and your own understanding of yourself.

Most beginners make up characters. They give them hair of a certain color, eyes with certain expressions, tall lean bodies or short dumpy ones. Once they're made up and described clearly, the new writer tries to force the breath of life into them.

They are straw men and wooden women! They can stay that way for a long time, too. But with the discovery of "I am the kind of person who," a writer finds gold—finds real people and knows how to get at them.

You, the writer, are a sort of springboard. You see yourself more clearly and begin to extend your vision to include other people. Not just that hair, eyes, and body structure. Not just that instinctive sensitivity and universality of our first needs, either. Instead, the writer filters other people through the question, "What *kind* of a person are you?"

So with actual living people around you, using your experience in trying to understand yourself on paper, you add another jigsaw piece to the puzzle of writing.

Set down a list of names. Your father. Your mother. Your best friend. All the people you think you know.

Then, choosing one name at a time, pretend that *you* are your father and that *he* is writing "I am the kind of person who."

Granted, when you're finished, they probably wouldn't recognize themselves because they're tempered by your ideas of them. But they're beginning to take shape in your mind and that can excite you.

Assignment

1. From the list you've made, do an "I am the kind of person who" for anyone who particularly interests you—or whom you'd like to know better. Be as complete and comprehensive as you can.

2. Taking that same person, go to the stream of consciousness. Only, not your own stream. Make it the way *he* would take in the world, catch *his* thoughts in that butterfly net. Make it *sound* the way he might say it.

Now we're ready to take a giant step. It really doesn't seem like one at first because you're still in the circle of self—and you're probably feeling déjà vu from filling out such things as college and job applications. But, believe me, this is *big*.

TAKING A CHARACTER HISTORY

You can do this right now. Be just as clinical as a doctor who makes out a case history. Make it brief—like a resume—just a sentence or so.

Assignment

Follow this form:
Case History of *Your Name*
A. Give date of birth.
B. Give place of birth.
C. Where did you grow up?
D. Describe your childhood surroundings.
E. What kind of a child were you?
F. How many people were in your family? Mother, father, sisters, brothers; name them all.
G. Chart your schooling.
H. What kind of work do you do—major, etc.
I. What is your attitude toward this work?
J. Are you in love? If so, how—romantically, happily, desperately, practically? If not—why not?
K. With whom? Describe the person.

L. Describe yourself physically and in full detail.

M. Describe yourself mentally, your odd quirks, likes, dislikes, aims in life, present attitude, and mood.

N. What is your problem?

O. How would you go about solving it in the light of what you've already said about yourself? In light of your entire being?

You can see for yourself. When you've finished doing only one "I am the kind of person who" about yourself, and you add to it the full case history of yourself, you know yourself a lot better.

Now, let's think about that other person of your assignment. As you've written his (or her) stream of consciousness, your knowledge has increased, and you've already done his (or her) "I am the kind of person who." When you've added to these your next challenge, you've very nearly lived inside the skin of the person whom you are studying.

Assignment

Repeat the above case history with the person you've already studied as the subject.

At this moment, then, with the above assignment behind you, you've taken that giant step we mentioned.

You have a character whom you know. You have identified with that person by finding what *kind* of character he is. You know that through "I am the kind of person who." You also know his background and his ambience and his problem. That's his case history.

And you've added to him his secret flashes of thought and feeling, and that's stream of consciousness. Give him total recall and what do you have? A full-bodied creation that is pretty nearly as real as you are.

But he has to do something, doesn't he? Here we don't want to stretch too far, or get involved with plot, which can be a different thing entirely. But we do want to investigate some movement.

"DEAR DIARY"

Everybody knows what a diary is—the reckoning of events, large and small, that total your daily experience. Sometimes, of course, they're studded with thoughts (stream) or remembrance (total recall) or self analysis ("I am the kind") or any or all of the things in your life (case history).

But for our purposes now—and because we've examined all these various helps to motivation, we just tie ourselves to the simplest method of action—almost like a calendar where you write down forthcoming appointments.

Assignment

1. Write, dating each day, seven days of diary, keeping only to the physical (external) things that happened to you.
2. Write the same seven days, but keep track of the physical (external) happenings of the character you've been studying.

Each step you have taken, from yourself to the other person, by showing how he thinks, feels, how he remembers his background and daily events, will enable you to know him well. You will know how he would act and react to various events and problems. Now you have *motivated a person*.

You are a sort of psychologist-minister-mother or father-teacher-lover, all wrapped in one package. And you are an objective observer at the same time.

You are also, whether you know it or not, a real writer. One more step and you'll be able to create characters for any story you may ever write.

Assignment

1. Think of a person who doesn't exist. Never met him. Don't know him. He's unborn and only in your mind. He's your main character. He's your *protagonist*. Make up a case history of him.

2. Write an "I am the kind of person who" for the character of the case history.
3. Write a stream of consciousness for the same character.
4. Write a total recall of him.
5. Write a week's diary (actions only).

When you complete these five pieces of work, you'll understand your lead character, he'll understand himself, and the reader will understand both him and what you, the writer, are getting at.

That's *how* you do it.

Sometimes a story opens with an "I am the kind of person who." Forgive me, please, if I quote an example from my own writing.

In "Reach for the Sun," a *Ladies' Home Journal* story, the narrator says:

> I suppose every fairly large family has somebody like me. I'm the one who made the "good" marriage. It brought with it a dependable man with a great talent for making money, a large house with pillars, and several acres of carefully tended ground. Trailing behind these three important factors were all the smaller luxuries which loom large to the average eyes. Cars and new refrigerators and garbage grinders and a full-time maid.
>
> The money made me the center of the relatives, I guess. That, and the fact that I'm tall and dark (or was, before the gray began to creep into my long hair) and everybody has always thought of me as regal.
>
> They also, let's face it, have thought of me as a bank charging no interest, a Lady Bountiful, or— let's face that too—a downright sucker on occasion.
>
> That doesn't mean I'm bitter. I love my brothers and sisters, and all of them started out with me in the simplest rural fashion imaginable. All of them have done well. But there have been times when they needed help. Those times they remembered very quickly that my husband Jed gives me a shockingly big allowance to do with as I please, and that one of my whims is to spread it around a little.
>
> I never figured out exactly what I thought. I helped where I could, without endangering their self-respect and independence. It was Jed's money, after all. There was more where it came from. It reflected no particular credit on me that I was known as sympathetic, understanding, and generous."

There is something concrete for you to work with. And it's a clear-cut case of "I am the kind of person who."

Assignment

1. With the above, go to stream of consciousness. Write those paragraphs as if you were the narrator letting thoughts pop in and out of her head as they pleased without the logical planning of the published piece.

Start with the sentences: "Why do they come to me? Jed's a good man—generous—kind—am I a sucker?"

2. The next effort goes to the case history. She is all there for you, except for the things you'll have to guess, to imagine.

Her name is Frieda. Start with that, and give her a last name. Follow the case history's steps in order. (Those things, incidentally, could easily bring you up against a story, and an entirely different story from mine.)

3. Do her total recall.

4. Now that you have the Frieda you discovered yourself—through her case history and her stream of consciousness—have her do something. Anything. Small. But make her do it in a way that only *she*—from what you know well about her now—would do it. See her. Feel her, in her dreams and wishes, and in your mind's eye. Bring her to breathing life.

That is where characters come from—full circle from yourself to Frieda. To any of them. Yes, some characters jump out, complete, whole and ready to be born. They have, apparently, been growing in the writer's mind for a maximum gestation period. When they are ready, they're ready! To write of them is pure joy.

I've heard writers say, too, "Crazy thing. I wasn't even planning to have this guy be anything but a minor cog. Then, suddenly, he begins to get life and speak for himself. First thing you know, he's taken over. He's the hero!"

Such a phenomenon is to be envied. Seldom does it happen though, and the writer who waits around for such miracles practically never finds them.

Most times a character is as reluctant as a shy boy at his first dance. He evades you. He distracts you. He changes the subject. He wanders off into the dark. He is frustrating and ornery and plain maddening.

When that happens there is the Stream, the I'm the Kind of Person Who, and the Case History. In any order you choose.

And you, the writer, are sitting in the boss-chair. As you should!

CHAPTER 13

Another Man's Shoes

What would it mean to you if somebody handed you a pair of shoes and said, "Look, these are another man's shoes. Put them on. Walk in them a little way. See where they pinch. And become one with all humanity"?

Hold out your mind, then. Take this—a motivating force for a deeper, richer life, a better writer. Something you can't read, or eat, or touch. Something you can only feel. But if you do feel it, you're going to be more than yourself. You're going to be everybody. You're never going to be alone again.

You're also—and most important—taking a giant step in the direction of being a writer.

When I was sixteen, at the railroad crossing on the way home from school, there was a tiny cubicle of a house for the watchman. Sometimes in the blustery winter afternoons we would walk home. Whenever we did, the old watchman waved to us. The flicker of a potbellied stove made a sort of warmth all around him and colored the dirty little window.

One Christmas I got a kind of religion. I wanted to do something for somebody who didn't expect it. I fixed a package of woolen gloves, scarf, and homemade fudge. I stopped at the little crossing house.

The old watchman opened the door. He smiled at me and I couldn't see any teeth at all in the pool of his mouth. The rest of his face rippled off away from that mouth in a myriad of wrinkles. He lost his eyes when his cheeks lifted.

I said, "Merry Christmas," and shoved the package at him.

The knuckles of his hands were very big and red and I was delighted with myself for having thought of gloves.

"Me?" he asked. It was funny how one word could seem to scrape all the way up an old throat, swim through phlegm, and come out clear and surprised.

I nodded.

He hefted the package, let his mouth close, and suddenly his eyes were there for me to see.

Much has been written about eyes, and who am I to add to it? It isn't enough to talk about dark depths, or warmth, or childish joy. Not when it's an old man in a crossing-house, with the smell of his stove and the smell of himself reaching out to pollute clean Christmas air.

Besides, how are you going to say that the earned wrinkles of his face were in his eyes? That sounds silly. But they matched. As if he had been given a wrinkle and a facet of light for everything he'd known of happiness and its opposite.

I smiled uncertainly, lifted my hand, and hurried back to the car. I heard him call.

"Wait," he cried. He stumbled on the slick highway and he looked like a moving black twig. He reached me and fumbled his hand toward me. He tucked what was in it into my hand.

I had trouble standing still. When you are young you are sensitive to the touch of age, of decay, of tomorrow-we-die.

"Merry Christmas," he said. "You buy yourself sometin' nice, huh?"

I wanted to give it back. But I didn't know how. So I just said "Yes" and "Thank you." I got in the car and started with a skid.

Through the rear-view mirror the old watchman got blacker and thinner and older until I went around a curve. But his hand was up, flipping like a fin, the whole time.

The dollar bill he'd handed me was folded into a tiny square. It was very dirty. It seemed to me that maybe it had been tucked into the greasy corner of black work pants for a long time.

It seemed to me that my gesture had been lost somewhere in the shuffle. That I had been topped.

Every year I bought gloves and scarf and fixed candy. Every Christmas, even when I went away to college, I stopped in with my package.

He had the dollar ready, and his face, too, watching me stop. He always said, "You buy yourself sometin' nice, huh?"

I never knew his name nor where he lived, and one Christmas there was a young, fat man at the crossing.

I rode right by. I didn't want the fat man to tell me what had happened to the old watchman. I knew.

Just as I have known all these years since, how it feels to be old beyond reckoning and not very clean, with nobody to talk to except a hissing stove—and to have a dollar in my pocket to give to a girl in a big convertible.

That was the time when I began to be a writer, although I didn't realize it for a long while.

For you, then, let me point out a simple and practical thing before we go on to consider why this big-little feeling—is so important. What we know and have known and felt for other people, as writers, is not just a happy and inflated ideal. It's something that people need, and will pay for, if we give it to them sincerely.

SYMPATHETIC MAGIC

In our normal daily life there is, among people of kindly intention and good will, a great deal of sympathy. Sympathy means "the act or capacity of entering into or sharing the feeling and interests of another; compassion and pity."

We feel pity for children starving anywhere around the world. We feel compassion for the family of a murdered man. We feel sympathetic toward (with that other definition which says that sympathy can be a "a reciprocal liking and understanding which arises from a community of interest and aims") an issue of the day, a cause, an ideal. We can also be sympathetic toward success, having an affinity for the desire to win, and in that measure enjoy the feeling of a Nobel prize winner, for instance. In reverse we're sympathetic toward the loser, having failed from time to time ourselves.

Sympathy is quite possible, quite easy, if you have those attributes we mentioned as necessary to the writer—sensitivity and universality.

But there is a finer and more accepted word for the feeling toward the old watchman. It is called "empathy." Empathy, defined, means the "imaginative projection of one's own consciousness into another being."

Empathy digs deeper. The person with this characteristic actually seems to suffer the children's pangs of hunger. Or wakes in the morning with the grief and anger of losing by violence the head of the family. Or knows, with an aching heart, how it feels to be black-skinned on any street, walking into a school, talking to any white person.

Empathy takes you up on the stage to accept that coveted award, closes your throat with nervousness, as you start to make the acceptance speech, and sets in you the wonder and humility that you should have been chosen for such an honor.

There is no creative field where this is not important, not accepted by the performer. The artist, behind whatever may come from his brush, or even his modern mobiles, feels something dark, gay, warm, or bitter. Not for himself but for the humanity he tries to portray. The musician walks somehow into the long-stilled heart of a composer and feels as that original musician did, and as the people for whom the composer spoke most likely felt. The actor, striding out on a stage—or shuffling or sneaking—is the height of empathy. By his body movements, his voice, his face not only does he transmit to his audience a character entire—but in order to transmit it he must *become* that person, bury his own personality, and have that character rise, Phoenixlike, from the ashes of that burial.

What is true then, for these other fields of endeavor, becomes the utter distilled truth for a writer. It isn't enough to *see!* You have to *be!*

You don't have to *be* in your personal life, of course. It would be a sad thought that there were as many evil, immoral, and hopeless people in the writing field today expressing *themselves* as there are evil, immoral, and hopeless characters in those same authors' books. Or that some of today's popular authors and playwrights personally sifted through the garbage that they collect on their pages and stages.

TO BE OR NOT TO BE

You bring yourself to your typewriter, yes. Your years of living. Your attitudes toward God and man and nature and history and all the rest of it. You can't possibly hope to write much of anything without those attitudes creeping up on the lips of somebody or into a description or a bit of narration. That's good, too, because it's one of the things that makes your work individual and separate.

But once at the typewriter, once involved in the birth of a story, or an article, a novel, or even an historical treatise or a term paper, you become a living symbol of empathy and walk in every man's—and woman's—shoes.

Fine, you say. But suppose, as human as I am, that I don't feel that way about the whole darned world. Suppose I'm much more concerned with my own looks, my own development, my own life, work, neighbors, friends, relatives? What then? Can I be a writer then?

The secret is, I'm much more concerned with my own personal life, too. It's more important that my husband be well and contented than the old man down the street. It's much more a concern of mine that my son adjust himself in a tough world than that another kid his age should succeed equally well. The welfare of Bang, our dog, is of more import to me than that of the barking little poodle who chases after him trying to start a fight.

I wouldn't be a human being if this were not so—and I'd be lying in my teeth if I pretended it were not so. It's the same with you.

Until you hit that typewriter or pick up that pencil.

WHO ARE YOU, REALLY?

Now, I am not a teenage bride, and never was. But next door to me there lived one. (Look around.) A blonde, heavily pregnant, and beautiful child, who had put away her pretty tight dresses and took all day to do the housework any older woman could have whipped out in two hours.

I watched her, laboriously finding her way in an adult world, and finally, I became seventeen. I was lovely and blonde and going to have a baby. I was alone and friendless in a place where there had always been friends and family before. I had nothing to look forward to, except a tired boy's arrival each evening from a job he despised, and which our marriage had forced.

When I was really she, I wrote my story, had my own birth pangs. And all the young girls from school came to give me a baby shower—and they left—they left—and I wrote:

> On the way to Balboa. To the blue above and the blue below and a week that belonged purely to all of them. The springtime boys and girls.
>
> It started in Jeannie's throat and she didn't know what it was. But it had to come out and it did. It came out shrill and loud and demanding.
>
> "Wait for me," she cried. "Oh—Mary—everybody—wait for me."
>
> She found herself running heavily, thumpingly, a parody of their lightness, down the stairs. She found herself halfway down those stairs, clutching the rail, her head bowed, sobs tearing her shoulders between the blades, the echoes of her screams filling all the stair well.
>
> "Wait for me! Wait for me! Everybody—anybody—wait for me!"
>
> The baby kicked her sharply, in reprimand.

The girl next door, coming to me with tear stains on her cheeks after reading "Wait For Me" in *Ladies' Home Journal*, called me "Ma" until the day we moved away.

I am not an old man in a nursing home, confused and lonely, a little dizzy from a shocking stroke, not able to express what is in me.

But after a visit there I wrote:

> I did not want to see from each doorway the eager, painful swing of heads, the sharp squashed hope on each face which found me stranger.
>
> I was stopped at the door by an old man in a wheelchair. He looked up at me out of eyes covered with fog. He asked in a voice as faint as far rain, "Will you kiss me, please?"
>
> I did, and, thank God, I didn't hesitate.
>
> All the rest of the day I walked with fury. I knew the man. I knew his son, his daughter-in-law, his proud quartet of grandchildren. I knew their civic place, their big home and social accomplishments.
>
> The nurse had asked me, "Will you come to see him again? Could you? Nobody comes to see him, ever. It's killing him."
>
> Not his body, dying, alone. That he could bear. His spirit, unwanted, discarded, dying in fragments because, in truth, there is no room for him.

I am still angry.

My anger, put into words as I put myself into the troubles of that old man, became a *Ladies' Home Journal* article, "Old Folks at Home." And the amount of mail I received justified the empathy.

I am not a college student, lost in a big university, trying to please his father by going hunting on vacation when all killing is repugnant to him. But I wrote:

> Riley dropped the bird suddenly, the weight too great. It fell like slobbered mush against the platform. He looked at it. Soft gray feathers, from white to dark. Great crooked wings. Long twisted neck. Blood, lots of blood.
>
> He looked at it. He waited. He waited to feel the nausea, the revolt of the belly and the mind. The guilt for the stilled heart and the spilled life's blood. He waited for a long time, his father still as a statue, waiting, too, across from him.
>
> Finally it came.
>
> It began with a tickling in his stomach and around his heart, a feathering against the back of

his throat, a stinging against the rims of his eyes, a
lifting of breath that choked him.

It was exultation. It was thrill. It was glory. It
was pure joy, untouched by anything but its own-
ness.

Nobody has bought "Sunrise Service" yet—and perhaps nobody
will. But for its eighteen pages, I *was* Riley.

BE THERE!

Do you see? What started back there when I was young, with the
girl on the trolley, with the old watchman at the railroad crossing,
comes forth to aid me—to set me in another skin, other shoes—when
I need to be there.

In the most commercial sense, it has furnished my income for a
very long time.

The same for you. You look at people with the priceless sympathy
and empathy.

Empathy can extend, and should, into the area of objects, too.

For instance, you want your reader to know how your character
feels about—let's say—a hidden velvet box. You can say, quite simply, accurately and dully, "He was afraid to find out what was in the
hidden velvet box." Or, "He was glad to be giving his lady pearls, as
he opened the hidden velvet box."

But if you can have empathy with that box—can feel it against
your palm, the softness of it—understand the intricacy of a clasp in
fingers that are either afraid or anticipating—and if you can put velvet and clasp into your own identification of them—you have it
made.

This same sort of consciousness must carry into the *area*, or *setting*, of what you're writing too. There is no better example than
Daphne Du Maurier, who most certainly must step completely out
of her luxurious and formal British world every time she sits down
to write. She steps into, with the greatest of self-transformation, a
long dark tree-lined lane leading to the haunted setting of *Rebecca*. Or
the midnight terrorized, shadow-split road of *Frenchman's Creek*.

I did not live in 1873. I never saw a sandstorm on the desert. I
wasn't a boy with a pony, a saddle, and a dream. But in "Pool of
Sand" in *Saturday Evening Post* I wrote:

A thing was happening, he noticed, brought back to himself and Bonnie by her slight nicker. Over the desert, as far as he could see, little puffs of dust lifted and whirled like tumbleweed. He felt no wind direct upon him, but the loose sand knew the breeze and frisked with it.

Each puff, wherever he looked, had the purple cast of early evening. The trail ahead of him seemed strangely narrower, as if it tightened itself to make a more rugged way into the foothills ready to curl through the mountains.

Bonnie made the slight noise again, a whimper like a sigh. Then, crashing down upon them both, integrating the dust puffs, aligning them into waves of sand swirling in all directions, came the sudden wind.

Dan was immediately blinded by it. He pulled down his hat and lowered his head as Bonnie's was lowered before him. The steady stream of wind and sand pushed against them both, savagely plastering his clothes to his skin and whipping them like pennants behind his back.

What should have been a long slow desert twilight was brown midnight. What should have been a sight of mountains was fuzzed out into sheets of sand. What should have been a trail was quickly, shockingly, covered over, thick-piled as blown snow on an open town street.

By the time that I was finished, I was literally more thirsty than I had ever been in my life, and spitting out sand.

This example leads to the next kind of walking in another man's shoes. This is walking into another era, and becoming one with it.

SECRET OF SUCCESS

We have before us always that classic of modern times that had more readers, more movie viewers, made more money—and continues to do so—than almost any other piece of writing except the Bible— *Gone With The Wind.*

Margaret Mitchell was the wife of an important and well-to-do-man. She lived in a present Southern world, far removed from any troubled Civil War era except through the memory of ancestors. Yet, as if she were involved in some weird incarnation, she managed to turn a switch that put her in the middle of those years and kept her there. Kept her among people who must surely have been more real to her at the moments of their creation than the tangible, living, everyday forms around her.

Her empathy was all-inclusive. She walked into the minds and hearts of her characters. She walked down the streets and byways. She went into the hospitals of a burning Atlanta, and through the horrors of the Reconstruction. She did not walk with Scarlett O'Hara alone. She fitted into many shoes, tattered or satin, marching or turned up in death. And every single character lived for the reader, and still does, complete, whole, breathing.

I do not believe that she deliberately set out to do this thing, any more than I have when it has worked successfully for me. I do not believe that you will, when you approach a story, an article or a book, precisely and wholly plan to scrape the surface, to fit the shoes, of every person you put into it. Any more than you would intend to write reams about what makes them tick psychologically.

But if you keep your eyes alive—to all people, seasons, small birds, animals—you'll find yourself writing not only *about* them, but *of* them, and *from* them when you add empathy. You keep your ears alive to the sounds of all kinds of voices, the tales they tell, the emotions they indicate or try to hide, and your dialogue will come in honest phrasing from lively lips.

Above all, the only way to learn to write in this fashion is to learn how to *care*. Not just what happens to the characters in your writing. But to care about what happens to living people themselves.

This caring is the great burden that all creative people carry in their hearts. Lots of people who are not creative carry it, too. They are the good neighbors, the warm friends, the true lovers, the world idealists.

Good writers are all of them, on paper at least, no matter how brusque or ivory tower or indifferent they may seem to be to outsiders.

It's never comfortable, never easy, never light-hearted, to care honestly. About a cause or a person or a dog. It is an underlying darkness to care, one way or the other, about everybody and everything. But a real writer cares, no matter what his shell.

And so must you.

CHAPTER 7

Description's Many Faces

There was a time in the field of writing when description was a sort of long bridge to stroll over until you leisurely reached the mainland of the story and it slowly unveiled before you. These were the good old days, when Doestoevsky could seat two young men opposite each other on the Warsaw train and use well over a hundred precious words to describe each of them.

"Broad and flat nose . . . high and well-shaped forehead . . . thin lips . . . deathly pallor . . . coarse and insolent smile . . . hard and sunken cheeks . . . thin, pointed, almost white beard . . . eyes large, blue, intent . . . something gentle though heavy, pleasing, thin, clean cut . . . though colorless."

And so he began *The Idiot.*

It was the good old time when Dickens, after a narrative hook, seemed to take a long breath and build a background, word by word, which covered half-a-dozen pages of squiggling; when Conrad, with a strong hand and generously splashed phrases, took his readers into far places and took his time doing it.

Those days, would-be writers, are over!

You, yourself, must know this well. You are trying to be a writer, yes, but you are also a reader. When have you had the feeling of peaceful meditation which allowed you to sit down with a thick book (unless ordered to for a course) and march slowly, steadily, with lack of pressure, into its pages? There are those dedicated readers of the classics (and I must confess I am one of them) who plan their time for the long gentle evening, to walk back in time and live there for a happy while. But as it is for you to whom words mean something, far greater is it for the average person, who reads on whim and wants to be right into the heart of things before anybody, or any TV program, can distract him.

FAST ON ITS FEET

The art of description, then, has changed mightily, even since the day of Du Maurier's *Rebecca* and the ride up the long road to the great house. It must be as of now, a subtle blending—an interjected sort of thing, a sly slipping-in of the small phrase, the right word—which will enhance and explain and picture. It isn't a simple task.

But in some ways it's far more challenging, just as writing poetry is, in varied fashion, more exciting than prose. The word used must be *the* word, and the search for it can be fascinating.

One thing to remember, first of all, is that description is not a fancy deal, nor is it separate from the body and content of the story. It is a process of interweaving. So that perhaps from a bit of dialogue we get a visual picture. From a sudden movement we see a whole form take shape. From a facial expression a whole mood is set.

Does this sound complicated? It's not, and thankfully, it can be learned. But first there are some things to look out for.

ESCHEW VERBOSITY

Most beginning writers fall into two groups when they try to describe on paper. The first ones go back to their early reading and those illustrious gentlemen we mentioned back there. They get verbose, which means merely "wordy." They get too rich with butter icing. Any reader's mind can take just so much of this before nausea sets in.

This was my trouble when I began writing and sometimes it still traps me if I don't watch it. I was (and still am) so in love with words. There were so many of them. They could be set into such thrilling patterns, or strung into such unusual, complicated lines. I was carried away with them; the sight, the connotations, sometimes even the rhythmic flow, almost heard in the back of my ear as I wrote.

I thought of orange trees, and didn't write, "They smell wonderful."

Instead, it was "the teasing, tangy, shaking, pervading, romantic, insistent aroma of their blossoms."

I thought of a beautiful face and didn't say, "It was pure and lovely."

Instead it became "a portrait done in oils of wisdom, dreams, love, and guilt."

I thought of a child, and didn't say, "She was a dressed-up little girl."

Instead, "Innocence walked abroad in a crisp full skirt trimmed with tiny rows of hand embroidery, clipping and swinging above small pink-shell innocent knees."

You know what I mean. Aren't we ridiculous? Aren't we flowery? Granted, a certain amount of this kind of experimentation will be good for you—to be carried away by it is fatal.

Experimentation is almost always good. How do you know how well you can do unless you sit down and let the stuff pour out? Writing is learning to see your mistakes so you may learn the wisdom of correcting them. Try first. Correct later.

But besides being careful, by trimming and watching, we can also be duds at description by not reaching far enough.

BLAH, BLAH, BLAH

You know well that we are living in a brusque and clipped age. Too many people seem to be afraid of any bright and shining phrase. The way they talk is called *pedestrian* (a word we'll deal with in *dialogue*) and is found in far too many of today's books.

This pedestrian business means just about what it says, whether description, dialogue, character, or plot. But for our purpose now it means that the description plods along as if it had sore feet, and is so normal, so usual, that it can't possibly excite either the imagination or the thinking of the reader.

You see, some people overflow with words. In your acquaintances I'm sure you know many of them—the sort who start talking like a plug was pulled out of their mouths or a dam broke. Other people just look at you and nod and never say a word except the simplest ones they can find.

When I was young, because I was pretty articulate and noisy myself, I had the deepest respect for quiet people. I always used to think, "Still waters run deep."

I had a very quiet friend. One evening, as he often did, he sat in the most comfortable chair and just stared at the ceiling. I asked, as I had a hundred times before, "What are you thinking about?"

He replied calmly, "Nothing."

I knew him five more years before I realized he was telling the truth. He never *did* think of anything.

Sparse description, aside from being pedestrian, often makes the reader feel that the writer has no vocabulary, either in words or thought.

For instance: the day was cold. She stood shivering: tall, skinny, blonde.

AVOID CLICHES LIKE THE PLAGUE!

The trap that makes for such dull description is baited on one side by terseness—and on the other by cliches. To say a sunset is a "ball of fire" is a plagiarism of some old somebody's, who many centuries ago was original enough to say it the first time.

You'll find as you write that many such phrases come to mind. "Hot as hell . . . cold as ice . . . tepid tea . . . tangled emotions . . . smooth as silk . . . black as night . . . pure as snow (usually driven) . . . full as a tick . . . high as a kite . . . young as springtime . . . old as the hills . . . bright as a dollar." The list goes on and on.

All of these are so overused that anyone reading them finds they don't even register. They just slide right through the eyes and out the back of the brain without taking hold.

A good thing to do, right now, before we even begin to talk about the various kinds of descriptions and how to sharpen ourselves in their use, is to make a little rule:

When a phrase comes immediately to mind, almost automatically and from a hidden source, *look out for it!*

Examine it carefully, to see whether it is fresh—or whether it has been said so many times that it's your first thought only; that you've dredged it up from wherever you keep old and familiar sentences.

Then—*hold it up a bit*. Let the *meaning* of the trite phrase be what you are trying to say. But search out a *new way* to say it. It doesn't have to be longer, or flowery, as we decried. It just has to be fresher, cleaner, with a little more glow than the words your reader has looked at and said himself almost forever.

On the other hand take care and beware, in this search for precision, that you don't sound like a telegram, whether in description alone or in your entire script.

"Jean!" Loud, sharp.

"Here." Slap, thud.

She fell. He stood over her. Tense, hating.

"Go." A shout. "Get out." A scream.

Don't laugh. It happens, and in far too many published works.

So how do we go about being descriptive properly? How do we strike the "happy medium" (see? Cliche!) between verbosity and sparseness? How are we descriptive at all if we can't take three paragraphs on every other page to tell about the house, the city, the sunrise, the faces?

How do we take the reader with us, most important of all, into the areas that will make him identify and become one with the background and the characters we describe?

Start by practicing physical description. And instead of limiting it to what can be *seen* alone—a sorry narrow practice—realize a great and simple fact.

We have *five* senses. We live each day in the world of those five, intermingling so closely sometimes that we don't really stop to find out where one begins and the other leaves off.

To train yourself in being precise, you cut a piece of pie from the whole of this physical description. You try to make it taste delicious with every bite, keeping it tied to *one* sense alone.

TAKE A LOOK, SEE

Consider, first of all, the sense of *sight*.

There's a lake. It's high in the mountains. You walk up a twisting path to find yourself suddenly confronted with the vision of it.

Assignment

Now—with that paper in front of you, that pencil—write five sentences only. No more. No less.

(Here's the discipline of *thinking* and *writing* on *demand* plus the extra discipline of *precision*.)

Tell what the lake *looks* like. Don't say one word of what you think about it, or how it smells, or any other sense except sight. Make anyone happening on your sheet of paper with the words on it, *see* the lake.

Is this difficult? Shame. Here are some phrases written by eighth grade students about that same lake:

The blue, beautiful, silent, shimmering water is
surrounded by pines. The green, crisp pine nee-
dles wave back and forth in the summer air. The
gentle lapping of the waves promises the ocean.
Along the edges, water grass contrasts with the
darker greens. And the lake itself looks as cool as a
glass of ice water.

And: A pass in the mountain lets the lake and the
sky blend into one. The trees come out to the water's edge. The far canyon reflects orange. The
green fringe of the border makes the lake seem to
lift up to where I am, and fills me with cool light.
The sun makes it both silver and gold, molding together.

Kid stuff! You can do much better if you try. When you have
tried, not only with a lake, but with any sight that comes to your
mind—the New York skyline, a baby asleep, an old lady—then you
move on to the next sense.

FE, FI, FO, FUM

Once again, the disciplined five sentences only. Once again, a pretend situation.

It's a snowy, cold day and you've been to a football game. You
walk into the house on Thanksgiving, ravished with hunger, rosy
from the cold, and the smells of the holiday dinner reach out to you.

Assignment

Write in five sentences only exactly how that house *smells* when
you enter. Nothing but odors.

Would you like to read what the children said?

I smell the soft, clean odor of the stuffing mixed
with the warmth of the flesh, the sick-sweet aroma
of jello. There is an almost-done smell, a warm
scent of anticipation. Something like a dozen cakes
and bakery shops at once. Suddenly there is also a
spicy smell, the pumpkin, the mincemeat. My
nose twitches with the teasing lift of coffee perking.

Pretty good. Top it if you can. Top it with perfume, or a slum street, or a flower garden, a pretty girl, or a freshly cleaned room.

NOW HEAR THIS!

It's county fair time (or carnival time or circus time).

You've parked your car and you're walking through the turnstile.

Assignment

Write five sentences about the *sounds* that reach you. The sense of hearing only, but so clearly that we can add visuals and smells to it ourselves, in our own minds, as we read it.

A boy named Ted wrote:

> I hear the rip of the ticket. The creak-click of the turnstile follows me. Next comes the rinkle-tinkle ring of the merry-go-round, and the sharp ear-splitting bangs of the fake 22s at the shooting gallery. Then I hear the roar of the flying dragon and the thwap of the bumper cars. The sad lost cry of a little child comes to my ears. Strange, but somehow it sounds like an overgrown department store on sale day or a busy city at noon.

There are many sounds to practice on. A quiet house at midnight, with the fear of an intruder. A ride on a noisy freeway. A voice whispering in love—or one crying out in anger. Make your own list.

MMM, MMM, GOOD!

The sense of *taste* now.

Let's pretend it's a blistering hot day and you've been working hard out in the sun. You reach into the refrigerator and pull out a bottle of your favorite drink.

Assignment

Try to write exactly how it feels on your tongue, in your throat, as it hits them. Five sentences again, and *taste* only.

Here's that ubiquitous eighth-grader again:

> The Seven-Up tastes like heaven on a hot day. A

> part minty lemon flavor is like a cool sweet drink
> from a flavored spring. The bubbles tickle my
> nose. A wonderful moist feeling comes as it passes
> down my throat, making it feel as though it were
> refrigerated with ice water.

IF IT FEELS GOOD . . .

That leaves us with the sense of *touch*. Let's have a dog—any kind
you please. Or a cat, if you're a feline-lover.

Assignment

Put your hand on the animal. Tell in careful words, again in those
five sentences, how the dog's fur or the dog himself (or the cat) *feels*
against your hand and fingers. Stick close to feeling only.

It helps to close your eyes for a moment, so that the sense of sight
is dimmed and will bring him to life as a blind person would.

> Like a satin blanket on my palm. A heated blanket
> that moves with the breath of the animal. A blan-
> ket with the shape of flesh and bone. One that
> grows suddenly cold as I move my hand forward to
> touch against the healthy nose. One that turns thin
> and wild with movement as I reach backward to
> outline the tail.

An eleven-year-old wrote that and it's especially good because it
stays with one simile—the blanket.

All children, faced always with new experiences, have fresh expressions. At three our son, at the shore for the first time, said of a
rising wave, "Like a mountain." When he walked into the water, he
cried, "Like a silky blanket." When thunder rolled, he trembled,
"Like a balloon goes bang." To him, even at that age, a banana
smelled "soft." Orange juice tasted "pully."

Perhaps to be truly descriptive, as in so many other phases of writing, we have to peel off the portions of adult skin and let the world
rebound against more tender childlike epidermis. Most certainly we
have to use total recall.

As a matter of fact, you'll get a great deal of help if you can peel off
your adult skin for all the senses. Try to train yourself to see and hear
and taste, smell and touch as a child would, getting the full impact of

each sense as if it were fresh.

Too often we go blind in every sense through life, simply because the familiar becomes the accepted, without enough attention paid to all things around us. To change this attitude is not a quick or simple thing, but it *is* something that can be recognized and learned. And it is in every way vital to the kind of communication we're searching for on paper. The *inside out*, *personal* movement of ourselves and our impressions into a verbalization that will invoke those same feelings in our readers.

MAKING SENSE OF IT ALL

There are five senses, then. To practice writing descriptions of each one of them is to increase facility, precision, imagination.

When that practice is accomplished, there is a further search.

Assignment

Take one background—say, a haunted house.

In those same five sentences try to tell how that house *looks*, *smells*, *feels*, *almost tastes*, *and sounds*. One sentence for each.

If these five sentences are done properly, and if you're fond of trying to write mysteriously, you have the beginning of a story. You have it so neatly that no reader is going to be bored with your description.

In any story, in any field, you may begin this way. Start with the physical description—how a thing, a person, a background, affects the five senses.

There are other kinds of description, though. These become more important as you gain writing experience.

One of these, used constantly, shows how a person *thinks*.

The other is how he or she *feels*.

These, of course, are the *mental* and the *emotional*. Almost always these two are so locked together that it's difficult to use one without the other, unless you're writing about a very cold-blooded and unfeeling human being. For most of you, just as in life, it's not easy to discover where the emotional ends and the mental takes over.

Obviously, this is even harder when you're writing, because you have to get inside of somebody beside yourself. With physical description, as we've discussed, you stay right in the comfortable area of how things look, feel, taste, smell, and sound to you and you alone.

But the state of mind of your characters is always of the utmost import in good writing. That state of mind of anybody you know, shared with you, tells you a great deal about him. So it is when you give stature to a person on paper.

Again, this is a thing that can be learned and it's learned by practice, by setting a situation for your character and climbing into his mind.

Suppose there is a young man. He's filled with ambition and has been working for a long time toward a position that is very special to him. If he should get it he'd be able at last to marry the woman he's engaged to, rent a decent apartment, or perhaps buy a new car to replace his present junker.

One morning in the mail he receives the offer of that job which will assure his doing exactly what he wants now and in the future.

He also receives another envelope. This he opens excitedly, still high from the news about the job. It's from his fiancee. It says that she is breaking their engagement—that she has fallen in love with someone else. And there goes the future and his strongest incentive. Here is a fine place to be a real writer. You can incorporate everything we've been talking about.

Do it with *contrast*.

Assignment

Again in five sentences:

1. What does he think when he sees the first envelope? What are his *emotions*—wondering, hoping, fearing, almost afraid to touch it, knowing that perhaps it can be a rejection of his dearest dreams.

2. When you've finished that, go one step further.
   How does he react to happiness?
   What does he think about the acceptance?
   Does he ride up high quickly?
   Or is it a slow satisfaction?
   Is he filled with disbelief?
   Or is he cocky, thinking and feeling that it's exactly what he's

always deserved?

(Incidentally, you'd know all of those things about his reactions instinctively if you had been working with him through total recall, stream, "I am the kind of person who"—and lastly, the case history.

3. For contrast now, turn to the second letter.

How does he read *it?*

Word by word with terror increasing?

Or in a gulp with a sudden horrible shock?

Or in anger?

Does he realize immediately that it is the end?

Does the knowledge, instead, seep into him, pinching his heart and closing his mind?

Does he shake inside and grit his teeth and get ready to bear his disappointment?

Or does he rant and rave and pound the wall?

Your questions and answers can go on and on, but each one of them, each in the field of *inner* description, serves the same purpose. It reveals the kind of person your hero is.

4. Now—add *physical.* For extra contrast, for adding a kind of rich- ness and poignancy, an extra tug on the reader's feeling, you can use those physical descriptions we just worked on.

Smell? The odor of bacon coming up the stairs from the kitchen perhaps—the known, the hoped-for, the treasured, to contrast with the insecure life that now faces him. *Write your own.*

Sound? The voice of his mother maybe, talking on the phone, or singing, so removed from his heartache. *Write your own.*

Sight? The letters in his hand, balanced against each other, white as snow, with all the words smudged and blurred and running into nonsense from his emotions.

Write your own.

Taste? Well, acute disappointment can easily have flavor, an acrid or bitter or sharp taste at the back of his throat. And tears, held tight by conditioning, can taste rancid. *Write your own.*

Touch? The thinness of the paper, such fagility, such smoothness, to carry that heavy a load. Sense of touch is often heightened, as are all senses, in moments of conflict. So, as he rubs his face he's aware of his beard. As he drops his hand, he knows the roughness of his sweater.

Write your own.

The description continues, as varied as the person writing it. There's only one big requirement, divided into these smaller specifics and that is to try to feel as the young man feels—and to make the reader feel it, too. That is empathy. That is universality. It doesn't take fancy writing. Or telegram style, either. It's just writing simply and as strongly as you can.

OFF THE DEEP END

If you walk steadily, one step at a time, you can cover a lot of ground, can't you? So now let's extend ourselves even further, into an area we really don't know very well. One you probably hope you won't know ever. Although this is an exaggerated example, the basic principle will be repeated again and again in any writing career.

You can't possibly live all of the lives you might want to write about. But you do want to write about many different lives. There's the next step, the next practice.

Assignment

Pick either a boy, man, woman, or girl.

Set him or her into a situation where he (or she) isn't thinking rationally. Where he's really off his rocker. Way out there; alone. Mentally disturbed.

Write a description of his thinking that will tell the reader exactly what the situation is, what triggered the state of mind, and how disassociated, illogical, remote from reality, his *thinking-feeling* is.

PRACTICE MAKES PERFECT

Extend yourself to as long as you like. Set your own situations and range as widely as you wish. How does a new child in a new town feel the first day of school? How does an astronaut feel the moment, or the night, before lift-off? How does today's pressure affect the parents of a juvenile delinquent?

Or if you like, stay personal for a while. How did you think and feel about your first kiss? Your first dance? Your first disappointment? How do you feel—and think—when you watch the six o'clock news? What sort of thoughts and feelings come to you when you witness a blatant injustice, a great play, a concert, a violent storm, a hospital ward? You take it from there.

Each of these phases of description may be used in nonfiction too; it incorporates the same depth, the same senses, characters, backgrounds, in short, the feeling of aliveness, which fiction does. Just because it contains factual material makes no difference in the approach, which is pointed out in later sections.

Assignment

Create your own situation and incorporate all types of description within it.

So, you see, quietly and slowly, with care, we add all these factors together. Just as you once practiced adding figures to a correct sum; or, to go back to our analogy, worked to put together a jigsaw puzzle.

When the practice is over, you'll be very close to becoming a writer.

This is what happens. You wouldn't be trying to write at all if there weren't some ideas—*from your own life* or from observation of *others*—that you need to express. It is logical after your practice sessions to go to a real life situation of your own—or one you've watched.

Assignment

Think of the *character*.

What does he *think* and *feel?*

Think of the *background*.

Show how it appeals to as many of the five senses as it will fit. Now—describe!

Start with the *background or setting* if you like. The weather. The time of day.

Inject your hero (or protagonist) into this background.

Give him a state of mind.

Make this state of mind relate to a problem.

(This problem is the situation that you wanted to explore in the first place, you know.)

By the time you've put all of your practice descriptions into use— sight, smell, taste, touch, sound, emotions, and mind—and have done it clearly, simply, concisely, with as fresh phrases as you can humanly find—you're off and away on a story.

A real story—the one *you* want to tell. Be *sure* to save this assignment.

CHAPTER 8

The Words in Their Mouths

"Why, how do you do, Mr. Ballaman? My, but you look perfectly charmingly groomed this morning. Out freshening yourself in the early air? That beautiful wife of yours, is she still as sweet and charming as ever? I never in my whole livelong life saw a lady so sweet and charming. She almost— not quite, mind you—but almost, deserves a fine gentleman like you!"

Yak, yak, yak. What kind of a person is that?

"Awright. Stick 'em up! One move and you're dead!"

And that?

"Don't want ice cream. Want cookies. Want balloon. Want candy. Mean mommy. Wahhhh . . ."

This?

"And so, my beloved friends, hold dear to you this rich admonition in the world of this spirit— this great exalted ritual since time eternal—this marvelous promise . . ."

You know him.

"Hold still. This will only hurt a minute. Take two of these every four hours and then . . ."

You've met them.

"I'm *dev*astated! I washed my hair and I can't do

a *thing* with it! And this new lipstick, it doesn't do a *thing* for me! Oh, dear, I just could *die!*"

Sure, she's an old friend, too.

"And—my friends—if I am elected—"

Him?

"Get L.A. for me, Doris. No, I told you, Jonesy! No raise! You keep that up, it's over and out, buster. Hello, hello, Van Huson? Cancel that order of the twenty-fourth and see that . . ."

Yes, you're right.

"Oh *mother*, you just don't under*stand!*"

I knew she would get in here somewhere.

I also knew that we'd get to this point sometime in our writing journey from inner space to the outer world. I've been putting it off a little because it's a broad jump ahead. But it's one that has to be taken before you really move your characters into action and a story.

Let's review what you have going for you along about now.

You know yourself and the source of all your thoughts. You know what you need in intangibles to bring them forth. You know what you have to face in hazards and hardships in order to write. You've learned how to remember backward, how to dig inward, how to analyze yourself. You've extended those patterns to study your neighbors, to find unknown people. You've searched for the best means to describe everything there is to know about any character you want to use.

Most important of all you've done all of these things on paper, in black and white, for the world to see. You have *written*.

In short, you're well on the way. Except, of course, that nobody, if he can possibly help it, stands mute and silent, saying nothing about anything. He has to have words in his mouth to communicate. And so does your character.

WHAT DID YOU SAY?

Right here is where you begin to be the eavesdropper.

Whether they admit it or not, all writers are exactly that. Sitting in restaurants, munching slowly, staring off into space, riding buses, leaning just a bit too close over the back of the seat ahead, relaxing on park benches behind unread newspapers, head cocked toward a neighbor.

These people could be crackpots, of course, and dangerous. But they could also be writers and perfectly harmless. Listeners-in on the world of speech around them, trying with a kind of desperation to record it mentally, praying that it will spring out, natural and right, from the lips of their characters at some future, needed moment.

Many fine writers have remained a species of essayists because they never learned to have that eavesdropping ear. Never managed to make people talk the way they should, would, and needed to, with complete ease.

Many a writer has gone lickety-split on the typewriter through every kind of character revelation, background, description, action and narration, only to trip and fall *thunk* at the first "she said" and "he said."

All writers occasionally have trouble with characters who remain stubbornly silent, like sulking children. Too few writers have thoroughly examined the fabric of this particular part of the craft. You've read them. The book is good—until somebody opens his mouth.

There are things to be avoided, first of all, if you're to make people sound like people.

You begin, believe it or not, by not letting them sound *too much* like people!

Think about it a moment. Picture for yourself two women meeting in the supermarket by accident, who haven't seen each other for years. Listen to them.

"Why, Mary Jones, imagine meeting you here."

"Why, Sally Smith, is it really you?"

"How have you been?"

"Just fine. How have you been?"

"Just great. Do you live in town here?"

"Yes. Bronson Street. And you?"

"Yes. Mercy Avenue. Been here long?"

"Six years. You?"

"Four."

"Are you married?"

"Don't make me laugh Married seven years. You?"

"Don't make *me* laugh. I've got three kids.

"Me, too. What's your married name?"

"Sanders. Yours?"

"Johnson. What does your husband do?"

"Insurance. Yours?"

"Mortician. How about we get together sometime?"

"I'd love it. When?"

"Oh, sometime very soon. I'll call you."

"Do that. We're in the book. Mercy Avenue."

"I won't forget. Gee, it's been great."

"Just great. So long. See you soon."

"So long. Luck!"

By this time you're sick to death of Mary Jones and Sally Smith. So is the supermarket manager who is standing nearby. Yet, this *is* the way people talk in real-life.

Pedestrian, it's called. The same word as we applied to description and for the same dull "sore foot" reason. It doesn't ride, or sing, or fly. It thuds along. It doesn't even move. And 99 percent of average human conversation is just that way.

What makes written dialogue synonymous with natural speech and yet different from it?

It goes somewhere. It can do many things to give a piece of writing life and breath.

SHOW AND TELL

Dialogue can show the *kind* of person the speaking character is. Remember the first few pages of this chapter. Take a peek back there.

Without any description and explanation, you know that the first speaker is a gushy, foolish woman who flatters everybody, and most likely has a needle up her sleeve for an occasional jab, too. Next up, not only because of content, but also phrasing, is a sharp and evil person—a robber or gunman of some kind. The third is a spoiled child, of course. The fourth, a minister and not a very good one. Five is our doctor friend. Next is a conceited woman thinking only of her looks. Then the usual politician, followed by the big-shot executive—hiring and firing, wheeling and dealing. And last, anybody's daughter—or son.

In such planning of dialogue (whether ridiculous or serious) much can be shown about the person who is speaking. The same thing happens in real life, even on first meeting. "How do you do?" "Howja do?" "How *do* you do?" "Hiyah." "Pleased ta meetcha" show some of the wide variety in even such a simple greeting.

Assignment

Here are a set of facts. Here are two people.

Show your reader, through their conversation, what *kind* of people they are.

Jane is a tall, homely, shy girl, utterly devoted to a very urbane, attractive man—she's his secretary. One night after working late (trite) he casually invites her to go out for a sandwich with him and offers to take her home.

Show how flabbergasted she is; how indifferent he is; how surprised he is at her excitement.

Do it in *dialogue*. If properly done, they'll come as clear as the situation-description could picture them.

INFORMING ON CHARACTERS

Dialogue can reveal *information*, too. Whenever it can be used for that purpose, it's a fine thing to do.

For instance: In a complete-in-one-issue novel, *Fast Train to New York*, in *McCall's*, I wanted to introduce the characters on a train so that the reader would know who they were. It seemed clumsy to walk down the aisles and peek in the roomettes, clumsier to have them come in one at a time, because there were quite a few of them.

So I simply had the heroine, after boarding the train, talk to the porter.

> "Anything you want, Mrs. Dean, anything whatsoever, you push that there button."
>
> "I will."
>
> "You get yourself a good night, now. All's aboard that's coming aboard. Two in L.A. Mr. Oliver, he snoring through the walls." The grin repeated. "Never take more than three martinis at the Biltmore, he tell me."
>
> "Are there many people in our car?"
>
> He held up a pudgy finger. "Miss Hubbins, she on at L.A. too. Look scared out of her wits. Four gets on at Pasadena. Rich daddy and daughter AND"—he managed to capitalize the conjunction—"Sonya Abbott and Tag Bailey."
>
> I thought of Jean, who read all the movie maga-

zines and who would jump with excitement if she were here.

"Nobody else pound down this aisle tonight."

He smiled his way out and rustled off.

There you are. In a short conversation we got the cast together as surely as if they had walked across a stage. And, with the porter's quick observations, showed something of the situation of each one.

Assignment

Use your imagination this time.

Choose your own people.

Gather them together anywhere you like.

Work out a way for the reader to meet them all in one swoop.

THICKEN THE PLOT

Dialogue can be used to great advantage to forward the movement of the plot, too.

Again from *Fast Train*. "Well, I thought—perhaps this afternoon"—he swung one hand out toward my letters—"you might be busy here. You could keep an eye . . ."

"An eye on what?"

He turned his own eyes away from me. "I have to see a man on business," he said fast. "If there were any possible way to avoid it, I would. I tried to make Sandra come with me, but she refuses. She says she going to stay here and nobody can budge her."

He looked at me then, complete defeat on his face. "Nobody can, either, by heaven. But if you were here—if you could maybe get her to talking, keep her interested . . ."

I listened to the things he didn't say.

"I had already made other plans," I began, knowing by the past tense that I had already discarded them. "I—I wanted some air."

Holmes Mitchell discarded something then. He discarded his pride. It was a terrible thing to see.

"Mrs. Dean," he said, "she got away from me last night. She—she got hold of some—" He swallowed. "I'll hurry back. If—if she can just be watched—for a little while."

I couldn't stand his eyes.

"I'll stay with her," I found myself saying.

In this conversation, while the train was switching in Chicago, the plot was forwarded in several ways. The heroine, a married woman, gave up her plan to spend the day with a man to whom she was attracted. It changed her direction. It tossed her into another situation, with an alcoholic woman whom she suspected of planning suicide. She rescued the woman from depression and also made some serious decisions about herself.

It forwarded the *plot*.

ON LOCATION

You can save a lot of fairly uninteresting writing by occasionally letting the conversation take your characters from place to place, too.

Instead of saying, "When the train stopped and I met Grady, I walked down the platform, down the steps, onto the pavement and began to stride ahead," I said:

> Grady was waiting on the platform.
> "Hurry up, ma'am," Plagus called from the pavement below. "Them washing machines going to get our way right soon."
> The ground felt strange under my feet. "It's as if we'd been on this train forever."
> "Let's walk fast," Grady said. "Let's go way up there to the end of the station."

So, they were in motion. They were off the train and heading toward a definite destination, all in a few lines of dialogue.

WHAT DO YOU THINK OF THAT?

One of the most important functions of good written dialogue is its ability to show the emotions of all kinds, the attitudes, and the background of any character. These may be done separately, of course, but often they are naturally combined.

An example of the same story:

> "Hah," she said. "People."
> I kept quiet.
> "Young love, I suppose." Her nice eyes were suddenly full of anger. "Boy meets girl, boy loses girl, boy gets girl. Only when he gets girl, he doesn't want her. Would that sell a story for you?"

I said softly, trying not to make an interruption, "That's been done."

"So it has," she said tiredly, "and recently."

"What's your name?" I asked, this time insistently.

"Ellamae Hubbins."

"Sounds like a big kitchen and apple pies baking and lilacs by the window."

"What it really is—" she clutched her purse tighter—"is a cold-water flat, a mother in a sanitarium and a father who used to be an important lawyer until he lost his courage."

"Sometimes," I said, "what we need more than anything is somebody to talk to whom we'll never see again." I nodded sagely. "Now, me," I went on, knowing from experience that a confidence breeds a confidence, "I'm sort of taking stock on this trip. My husband and I—it seems to me we've been growing apart for a long time. Each day, each week, a little further apart."

Ellamae Hubbins said, "Hah," again and brought me from my thoughts. "I've talked and talked. I'm all talked out."

"To whom?"

"Doctors. Do you know what a nervous breakdown is?" Her words tumbled. "I had one. It takes a long while to get over one—" She began to shake.

I put my hand over hers. "Let's have a cup of coffee and forget all this seriousness."

"I'm afraid of people again," she whispered, bending her head over her locked fingers. "I got all over it, you see. And Johnny had this good job in California."

I let the silence wrap her, hoping it would make her feel secure, alone. It did.

"Then my father died." She shook her head. "There was insurance. Quite a lot of it. Imagine, a cold-water flat and defeat all those years. But he kept up the insurance. And I never knew."

"He must have been quite a person."

Again that shake of the head. "No. Yes. I don't know. I can't picture him any more."

"And Johnny?"

The anger was in her eyes again. "People like Johnny can't wait for nervous breakdowns. Maybe if the . . ."

Let's think about the content of this dialogue for a moment and consider what it holds.

Everything mentioned so far, right?

It reveals the cast of characters, the kind of people they are.

It informs—Ellamae's name, her background, her problem.

It forwards the plot, because Ellamae shows that she could easily be the suspected suicide-threat.

It shows the emotional state of Ellamae, her desperation, her disillusion.

It shows her general attitude toward her troubles.

These five things then, are the main duties of dialogue. If you follow them, your dialogue will be true to the way people really talk. But it is a distilled kind of speech that filters out the dull and dross. It won't be pedestrian, either. When you put revelation, information, plot, location, and attitude into the conversation of your characters, you have a certain focus.

You are more concerned with *what* they have to show than in *how* they speak. Somehow this seems to take the strain from the whole process and they begin to talk well and as they should in each case.

A SMALL REMINDER

When you write dialogue, *do not stop the action to let the characters speak.*

You have seen the plays where, sometimes for lack of good direction but often for lack of good writing, everything comes to a sad halt while the actors stand around and "talk things out." They don't "walk on their lines."

Your characters must walk, move, have their being as they talk. And for pity's sake, in between sentences, give them something better to do in the way of action than to "light a cigarette" or "pour a drink."

Keep speeches short.

People, except in rare cases, do not speak in long sentences. There's always the interplay, the attempted interruption, in real conversation.

Don't be either high-flown, or too intense or accent unimportant talk. Keep it simple, distilled, but straight-forward.

There's an old saw that is a perfect example of *high-flown*. "My intended's mater warned us never to engage in any premarital interdigitation."

Sounds very important, doesn't it? Even sexy. Well, all it means is, "My fiancee's mother warned us not to hold hands," believe it or not.

Romantic novels are often filled with dialogue that is too *intense*.

"My dearest of all beloveds, I worship the dust which is stirred up by your little feet, and the views upon which you set your azure eyes."

Yikes!

Unimportant talk really speaks for itself, but imagine if you can the woman who, staring at her murdered husband says, "I was buttering his toast."

Avoid spelling out accents or colloquialisms.

"I jes doan unnastan' mistah." Or, "I brek the aigs, un by un." They're hard reading. Typical, easy phrases, properly spelled, will give the same effect.

Try not to get hooked on "he said" and "she said." Search for better words.

"Your eggs are cold," he *sighed*. "Cigarette," she *snapped*. "That's good," he *snickered*.

You can see in each case with the word substituted for "said" that something is revealed. Sadness about the eggs, anger with the cigarette, and a joke with "snicker."

One great trick is not, unless you have too many characters going for you, to use "say" at all. This is easily done when there are only two people or instead you can use a fragment of action. Thus:

> He smiled. "Two way up front."
> I smiled back at him. "I'm not sure I want to."

Or:

> He nodded. "Doubt it though. Several empties up there." He glanced at my brief case. "You a buyer?"

I shook my head shyly. "I—I write."
Small words, but they keep the action going.

Assignment

Find a short story in a magazine, or pick one of your favorites, even a fable or fantasy type if you like.

Pretend you're back in the old days of radio; before it became the disc jockeys' domain, it was the greatest proving ground ever for dialogue. All action except for sound effects, every bit of characterization, emotion, plot movement, had to come from those words in the mouths of the actors reading the scripts. Only the narrator was there to fill in changes of location. Otherwise, the radio writer was on his own with nothing to juggle but dialogue. Try to be that writer with your short story. (You can get extra help here by borrowing some tapes of the old radio plays from your music library. Or listen to radio drama on your public broadcasting station.)

Assignment

Enlarge a radio script.
Put it on a stage, any kind of stage.
Add to the dialogue.
Describe the *setting*, the *appearance* of the characters, some of their *qualities*.
Move them about the stage with directions, just as you want them to act.
Try to keep them walking on their lines.

Suggested Reading

The book form of any of your favorite plays. This will give you an idea of the physical plan for a play, and how cast description and direction are pointed out by the playwright. Of course, the best aid here is to go to some plays or even a few rehearsals of a small local group.

Assignment

Give yourself a further dimension.
Make your stage play into a television skit. The action can range farther than on a stage. It can go inside and outside with cars, stores, people passing in the street, all sorts of backgrounds.

Assignment

This is an elective.

If you're still unsure and need more practice, take your story wide screen, full color, into the prodigious spread of a movie. Here you have the whole world and its peoples for a panorama. Add this breadth, *still concentrating on dialogue, mind you!*

Assignment

This is an elective.

If, in the midst of these assignments, you've been toying with a story idea you can start this whole process now.

Write a short story yourself.

Make it a radio skit.

Make it a television skit.

Or—make it a one-act play. Who knows, perhaps it will be good enough to get college production!

If you take the time and trouble to do these projects, you'll find that you're well into the freedom of the *story world*, which is even larger than the movie screen. It's as broad as your imagination and you can do as you like, go anywhere you want in one sentence, one paragraph, or one small piece of well-written dialogue.

Never lose sight of your original premise. *Know your characters* first. If you're sure of them, they won't let you down in this area, either. They'll talk with the intelligence, the flair, and the personality that is uniquely their own.

And they'll never be dull.

P.S. Keep in mind again here, that nonfiction, to be successful, very often is brightened and heightened by the use of dialogue. And not just in the direct interview area, either. Mastery of the spoken word is as vital in every field of writing as a campaign speech is to a politician.

CHAPTER 9

How Do You Really Start?

Well, the characters are behind us. What there is to know about them you've thought of, and tried, and learned. Now you're ready to walk into an entirely different but integral part of writing.

When you're learning to write there's hardly a thing you do concerning paper and pencil or typewriter that won't advance you. You're bound to become more fluent. This is true even if you have been writing for years, as a matter of fact. But there are times when both words and ideas seem to elude you. That's when you need some wise little tricks to move forward again.

THE IDEA BOOK

This *idea book* is not a diary with bits of descriptions, thoughts about people or life, or personal philosophy. That kind of journal is a fine tool, like the *stream of consciousness* for examining your own attitude toward life and writing.

The *idea book* is much simpler and far more useful. It's just what it calls itself: a list in a notebook of random bits of ideas that may, someday, like bulbs in the ground, develop into full-fledged plants.

It can contain anything. Just a good title. A passing thought. A mood. A tip of a head. The way a hand reaches out to shake yours. A clip from a newspaper. Anything. It's seldom an entire sentence; sometimes you don't even seem to be getting your wear out of it as you go back and take a peek once in a while. You've forgotten half of the ideas; somebody else has written the other half while your back was turned.

I've kept such a list for over twenty years. My whole career in writing, as a matter of fact, began with the first germ of an idea I set down in a small notebook.

A long time ago I sat in a restaurant, sipping the last of my coffee, taking my time, looking around.

Through the door came three people, a man, a woman, and a small child whose arms stretched full-length to cling to the adult hands. They found a table and settled down, laughing and talking.

The child was the focal point, not only of their loving glances, but of almost everybody in the place. Tight yellow curls, brilliant blue eyes with black lashes, a flower mouth, creamy skin—she was a three-year-old to dream about.

Flanked by her mother and father, though, she was startling. Those two, the man and the woman, were the ugliest human beings I had ever seen—distorted, caricatured. Nothing was right about them at all. Except the hot, wonderful, happy glow in their eyes as they looked at the miracle they had created.

I was touched. When I went home I pulled a dime store notebook toward me and wrote "Story Idea." Under the heading I put down "Homely parents with beautiful child."

I don't know now how many years it sat there, one forlorn little thought, a hint of an idea. All by itself.

This is stage one of how to get started. Don't let those delicate little bits of ideas get away from you. Write them down. They'll wait till you're ready.

Step two, for me, came when I had a moment of quiet and was reading a poem by Thomas Campion, a sixteenth century writer. I don't remember the first part of it, but I'll never forget the last two lines.

"Give beauty all her right," he wrote, "She's not to one form tied."

VARIATIONS ON A THEME

Quite suddenly my one notation in the book came into my mind. The idea-thought sparked the poem context. I had a *theme*, though I didn't realize it at the time.

A theme is not a plot. It is not a story, in any sense of the word.

A theme is, instead, the big general meaning behind a piece of writing. It is, if you want to put it that way, the moral of a story. Or the point of it.

And it can usually be distilled in one sentence.

The theme, then, of my first story idea based on idle staring at three people was identical to that of a famous old poet in the 1500s. There is such a thing as *inner* beauty. Anything could hinge on that one sentence.

So you begin to train your eye, or your mind, to see the *theme* behind almost everything you read. Or look at. Or overhear. It's quite simple to do and is often fun. On many occasions it gives you the essence of a situation, an essence its creators are probably unaware of.

There's a way to explain this essence, this theme.

Most mystery stories clearly imply that crime does not pay.

The theme of westerns is that the Good Guy always wins over the Bad Guy in the end.

The theme of *Gone With the Wind* could be interpreted as "all people have their own strengths in their own different ways."

The theme of Hamlet (so often discussed and analyzed) *might* be that *indecision leads to, and increases, all troubles.*

This is an action you can practice in your mind or on paper.

What is the theme of "Peter, Peter, Pumpkin Eater?"

What is the theme of this little book itself?

What is the theme of the New Testament?

For Extra Credit:

What is the theme of your daily newspaper?

What is the theme of Higher Education?

It doesn't matter where you look, you can find a theme behind what you see. Any piece of writing, no matter in what area, is a razzle-dazzle of undirected phrases unless there is that basic meaning and you understand it before you begin.

Perhaps it might amuse you to check my idea book and see what happened to some pretty skimpy thoughts.

1. Tomboy (me, really) first kiss . . . "It's Not So Bad To Be a Woman," *Saturday Evening Post.*

2. Two young suitors both give a young woman (me) flowers for party . . . "Posies for Pamela," *Ladies' Home Journal.*

3. Boy heavy sleeper (my husband) . . . "The Sleeper," *Collier's.*

4. Parents seeking time alone (casual remark from friend) . . . "Time Out for Marriage," *Saturday Evening Post.*

5. Woman whose saleman husband only comes home weekends (friend) . . . "Life Begins on Friday Night," *McCall's.*

6. Mystery suicide note on fast train (me on trip to New York) . . . "Fast Train to New York," *McCall's.*

That's what they call a random sampling in television polls, isn't it? But two things are evident and somehow well worth remembering in the above. First, most of them came out of my own experience—or if not, in experiences of people I know, and all of them, actually, were recalled. Built up, yes. Fictionalized, sure—but remembered first.

So don't let them slip—no matter how long they stay in your small book. You never know when a bulb will turn on as you check them over and light will flash on a path that you can follow to make them entire instead of just ideas.

Assignment

Get a small notebook.
Write in it any ideas you may already have collected in your mind. Look around you for others.
When you have even one or two, try to find a theme for each of those ideas. Jot it down beside them.

What good does the idea or the theme do? How do they get you started?
They spark the next step.

BAIT THE HOOK

This next step is the *narrative hook*. This is almost a self-explanatory phrase. A good *narrative hook* is just a beginning sentence, or paragraph with enough zoom in it, enough promise of something exciting or interesting or dramatic to come, enough quick sympathy with a person or a bit of dialogue, so that the reader will, literally, be *hooked* into reading the rest of the story.

To work with narrative hooks when you don't know how to begin a story or precisely what you want to say is a matter of practice, of trying different ones until you hit *the* right one. Usually you'll recognize it. But sometimes you don't. One of the big pitfalls of writing a story, article, novel, play, even a letter or a class theme, is that of getting off on the wrong foot.

Be warned in advance. There are two dangers to watch for concerning narrative hooks. The wrong direction. And too slow a start.

WHERE DO I GO FROM HERE?

If you start writing in the wrong *direction* and after a couple of paragraphs the words steady down and seem to march right along, before you know it your tangent is nowhere near the story you want to tell.

There's nobody to point this out, of course. The whole bit reads well enough. You can work a full day, a week, sometimes even to the end of the piece, before you discover what you've done. Sometimes you never do discover it until you turn it in or send it out and get that sad speedy rejection or low grade. And you wonder why.

There's nothing to do but tear it all up and start afresh. Which accounts for the crumpled pages around the writer's desk. For bad dispositions, too, and often for giving up the whole effort.

All because you didn't start right.

Here's an example:

I wanted to do an angry piece with a viewpoint I had already queried an editor about. But I started down the wrong road.

I wrote:

> I am a fairly quiet, peaceable middle-aged
> American, and a woman at that. Yet, suddenly,
> talk about 'Angry Young Men'! There's a horn of
> anger blowing in my ears which makes theirs
> sound like a peanut whistle piped in a strong wind.

It sounded all right at the time. I kept on going. I had set the article within the realm of my personal *emotions* and I was forced to stay there. I was *angry*. And angry I had to be in every sentence.

I had to keep topping myself. You've heard it on stage or TV. A scene, or an announcer, starts at the top of the lungs. There's nowhere for the actors to build, except to get into the area of wild screams. So I did, in every direction, taking off here and every whichway, noisy and hysterical. And I never realized it! The rejection read:

> She has involved herself in a melodramatic pre-
> sentation, which is not always easy to follow, and
> instead of pinning down all her complaints as com-
> pletely as possible, she has wandered all over the
> lot, probably touching too many subjects for a sin-
> gle magazine piece."

Wow!

They liked the idea still, though, and I used my second chance this way:

> Who's at the mercy of fools? Well, I'll tell you
> who is! The middle-class, middle-aged American,
> who is pictured always as frivolous, stupid or ugly.
> Who doesn't fit. . . .

And I was off and flying.

I was out of my own skin, so I could stretch. I spoke for a section of America and thus had wider range. The opinions were still mine, angry, a little controversial, but because of the right narrative hook I could be objective instead of being so personally and emotionally involved.

Remember this danger and my sad example. It isn't enough to practice writing narrative hooks. They have to be successful ones, setting the tone of your whole story or your article.

DON'T BORE ME WITH THE DETAILS . . .

The second danger is minor by comparison, and has to do, as does description, with the pressured age in which we live.

Reading has greater competition than at any other time in history. Somebody picks up a magazine in a supermarket, flips through it, sights a couple of beginnings, and either puts it back or buys it. Depending on one simple thing.

How fast did those two beginnings catch the interest? Were they more fascinating than the evening's TV programs, the movie at the neighborhood theater, the planned picnic, golf game, PTA meeting, bridge club, bull session?

You have three things to do to start any piece of writing. Remember? Idea book. Theme. Narrative hook.

You're just beginning to learn to put a story together, having investigated characters and become pretty good with them. You don't really have that idea book yet, nor any theme great or small. So, you go about writing narrative hooks themselves. When you're filled with ideas backed by powerful themes, you'll know how to start.

In this business of getting a story started, it doesn't matter how new or how old you are to writing. You can never get enough of being *specific and precise*, of knowing exactly what you want to say.

So to begin your practice, you make use of a simple basic rule of newspaper reporting.

QUESTIONS AND ANSWERS

The first thing a cub reporter is told is that space is valuable. Then, that the reader hasn't much time to spend. Next, that the reader wants to get the whole gist of the story as soon as possible. Which, of course, in many ways applies to all other writing—and reading.

This cub, then, is taught to include *in the first paragraph* the answers to the questions who, where, when, what, why, and if possible, how. Sometimes in that order; more often juggled at the reporter's discretion.

The exciting thing is that if you ask those questions of *every* narrative hook, one or more of them *can't* be answered!

This is the element that holds the *seed of the plot*.

Sometimes it is one question, sometimes another. But it always will lead forward and clarify the plot. Sometimes it even sparks it.

Assignment

May I suggest that you do this assignment before you read the examples that follow them. Below are two themes.

Write a narrative hook that answers those questions we mentioned.

A man dies suddenly, with many loose ends left behind. He's given a day of grace to come back and settle them.

A woman kills herself and doesn't leave any clue as to why she committed suicide.

Don't try to get those answers all in one sentence. Allow yourself a paragraph and try different openers.

Now, compare them with mine.

In "Day of Grace" in the *Ladies' Home Journal*, I began it:

> The thing with Mr. Ditterman, of course, was that he hadn't expected to be dead. Death, like a rocket trip to the moon, was far removed and utterly fantastic. After all, he was only fifty-one and in the prime, so to speak, what with golf in the summer and handball two evenings weekly all winter. Even so, it wasn't dying that bothered him so much. It was the speed. Jet-propelled, you might almost say. He said it.
>
> "It was too fast for me," he tried to explain to the Voice in the big red leather chair. "I am, by nature, a neat man. I don't like all the dangling odds and ends I left behind me."

Who?   Mr. Ditterman. (And just in passing always take time to find a suitable name for your character as you plan his life and his tale. You can use a directory, a phone book, or a book of names, but if you know your subject well, often a name just comes.)

Where?   Someplace in limbo or heaven or whatever.

When?   Right after Mr. Ditterman's sudden death.

What?   "What" can always be several different things. Here it is Mr. Ditterman's displeasure with the manner of his dying.

How?   We don't know "how" exactly he got there—but we presume an accident, heart attack, any quick death.

Why?   "Why" is almost always the most important question you ask. Here it is important to the plot—his need to go back and tie up those loose ends. A surface "why" would be that he's no longer living.

In the second part of the assignment, the *theme* was part of a long story in *Alfred Hitchcock's Mystery Magazine*, called "Three Case Histories." It began:

> It has always seemed to me that one of the cruelest things any person can do to those around

him (or her) is to kill himself (or herself) and lie there dead and gone beyond all questioning, with no suicide note on the table, or pinned to a pillow case, or in a safe deposit box.

Who?	There are two "whos" here. *Who* committed suicide? *Who* is the narrator, who thinks it's cruel not to leave a note?
Where?	The location of the finding of the body.
What?	The suicide itself.
When?	Not immediately revealed, so this question is part of the plot.
How?	Another unrevealed question and answer, and important part of the plot.
Why?	Again, this is the question it takes the whole story to answer. So it must be hidden carefully from the start, to be revealed only at the end.

(Incidentally, you can see that once you get inside the field of the suspense or mystery story, you hide those six questions, some or all of them, for as long as you can, letting just a little about them leak out at a time. But you ask them, all the same, and for good purpose. By their answers, you must outwit, out-plan and out-think the reader.)

Well, that assignment was narrative hooks. Given those one-sentence basic themes, working independently, you could be off on entirely different stories. One of the happiest things about hooks is their variety—which, conversely, is their most frustrating quality.

THE WRITE QUESTIONS
Those six little questions will stand you in good stead, quite aside from beginnings and in many other ways.

They will serve to *clarify*.

You may use them in reference to the *story*, as we have here.

You may refer to a character and ask those pertinent questions about him until he comes more sharply into your vision.

You can ask them of a situation, a background, an idea.

You can, if you're still a little unsure of your own writing dedication, play around with them and answer personal questions.

Why do I write? About *what* and *whom* do I want to write? *How* do I want to write? *What* do I want to share, to talk about, to give? *When* do I write, the best time, the hours I think and feel most alert? And *where* shall I write?

THE HOUSE THAT JACK BUILT

By now you must be aware that it's an interweaving process, this business of trying to write.

"This is the thought that stirred up the theme, that gave me a hook for a story."

And occasionally the pattern, as you practice, will become reversed.

"This is the hook that gave me the theme that stirred up the thought for a story."

For instance, sometimes you find that you've written such a dashing, exciting narrative hook that it cries for a second paragraph and a third and people, a plot, a climax, and a windup. If you allow yourself total freedom in practicing this kind of writing, you never know where it will lead.

In writing classes for children around eleven or twelve, the students came up with some narrative hooks worthy of attention.

"As Alice crept through the dark house to answer the phone, she felt like someone was following her."

Here you have no previous thought of idea book or theme. You just have a beginning, but the kind that makes the reader want to know more. Why did she *creep?* Why was the house dark? Why did the phone ring? Who was calling? Was someone really following her? What was she doing there, anyhow? How did she get there?

Another: "Splintered glass and an explosion made the night fall to pieces."

What splintered the glass? What glass? Where? When? What time of night? What exploded? Who was there?

"A gun cracked in the distance. A man cried. Then came silence."

Who shot the gun? Who cried? Was the man hurt? Why the silence—and again, where, when, how?

And then there was a classic, which I've always liked. "Buzz, snap, blutter, thud, I got it!"

I've stayed curious about that one. Who's "I"? What's buzzing? What happened when "I" got "it?"

Assignment

This time, follow through from the beginning.

Take an idea from your idea book.

Give it a theme and write the theme out in one sentence.

From that theme, write the best narrative hook you can, from your secret knowledge of what you're planning to do later.

Plot a story.

Assignment

Write five narrative hooks for their own sake.

Choose the one you think is best.

Study it for theme.

Write the theme in one sentence.

Galvanize that into the action of a story and you can plot from there.

Hang on to your idea book. The second assignment can get a little muddled from time to time. Then you can always come back to the number one spot, and write down the primary basic thought that your narrative hook has inspired. You can always work on it some later, better time.

P.S. It occurs to me that, by sticking to business, you were left up in the air about that first idea, theme, narrative hook story of mine regarding inner beauty.

I finished it. I called it "Beauty's Right." With my heart in my throat I mailed it off to the *Ladies' Home Journal*. About a month later there was a letter in the mailbox. My heart was in my throat again and my hands were shaking, too. I ripped it open.

It said: "Happy to buy" . . . and a price that was more than I had ever had at one time before.

I went temporarily blind and couldn't read the rest of it. I fell off my bicycle and skinned my knee on the way back home. My husband had to read it for me.

And at last, after the tough tag-of-the-Depression years, we had the money for the down payment on the little house we had so wistfully watched being built. Because out of a slush-pile of thousands of stories, some reader looked at mine—and liked it.

I tell this because some reader, somewhere, is still looking, despite the years between, and because—never doubt it—as you work hard on learning to write, this great, blinding moment could happen to you.

CHAPTER 10

You Must Have Plot

The human mind is a strange and wonderful thing, as has been noted by philosophers, psychiatrists, theologians, and writers from time immemorial. Sometimes it gets distracted and is so lazy that you're afraid you'll never get it going again.

Sometimes a writer's mind has a sort of "suicide wish" that he has to fight from the beginning of his efforts. You've heard stories about how authors sharpen pencils, make phone calls, read newspapers, find garbage to empty, take long aimless walks. They're true.

Such a wish is not just the claim of writing. It can be applied to almost any creative art—to the young actor who keeps putting off lessons, or going to auditions, to the young painter who takes long walks when he should be working, and to the pianist who does scales over and over to avoid learning a new sonata.

It would take several psychiatric sessions to probe every reason for each person's procrastination. Sometimes it seems as if they're afraid of finishing a task, or of success or failure if they do.

But many, many writers are afflicted with this. Not just the ones who take a dozen different courses and never explore their craft thoroughly. Any writer. The moment of truth is always tough to face.

There is also a deeper, more subconscious battle going on. Way at the back of your mind you have an idea. You have that theme. Occasionally, it's pretty clear. More often, it's vague and dim. But you have it.

You also, many times, have a definite plan for an ending, what you really want to prove. At the same time, you may have a good clean, sharp narrative hook beginning.

But in between is the story. The *plot*. The things that must happen to forward the theme. Many a writer has killed his talent young and undeveloped rather than face this dragon bravely and defeat it.

This is true. Anybody—well, practically anybody—can sit down and with a little dreaming and thought bring forth a few pages of description. Almost anyone can write a little vignette, a small incident, about something that he has observed or which has happened to him. Dialogue, or lesser conversation, can be handled by the pure amateur if he has a good ear for the way people talk.

But to start with that narrative hook which moves the story ahead; to use always the verbs and nouns and descriptive phrases that are alive and unusual; to have every bit of movement—mental, physical, emotional—of tight value to the forward movement; to make characters take on flesh and life by what they think and feel as well as by what they do; never to stand still or bog down in explanations; to get into a story the feeling of inevitability, that it couldn't have happened any other way; to stretch to a high point of a problem with everything snarled and unanswerable and then to unwind and unsnarl and answer—*all by having something happen*—is the big job, the nasty menial job, which defies and sometimes defeats the writer.

PLOTS AND PLANS

How to plot must be reduced to its simplest common denominator so that the basic learning of it will be right, like a beginning breast stroke, or a golf swing.

There are outlines, of course. They can be used to good effect and are by many workers in words. But you can be just as stymied by 1, 2, 3, 4, as by a blank sheet of paper.

So, there is instead the logical progression and a series of choices and questions. As always, you look inside yourself to find the answers.

Assignment

Is there a picture on the wall as you read this? If there isn't, find one, or go where there is one.

Here you'll plot something you really haven't planned to say, working on demand again.

Look at the picture. Think about it.

Give it a theme. One sentence. What is the underlying point of the painting? What did the artist want to get across? Perhaps it can synchronize with your theme.

Is there any kind of moral that can be drawn from it?

Still thinking about the picture, but writing this time, describe it physically.

If there are people in the picture, decribe them. If it's just a land-scape, invent people and set them into the frame.

You now have a place, a setting, a background. You have characters.

Jump right in and make them *do* something. What? Anything. Just get them into action.

Then, begin to plot.

You do this by a series of choices.

These choices are no less important when you're starting than when you've written for years; you're always faced with them. From paragraph to paragraph, page to page, the working writer must always make decisions, one after the logical other.

TAKE YOUR PICK

Picture a tree in your mind. Suppose you put a young man in the picture. Suppose he climbs the tree.

1. When he climbs the tree, does he fall out and break his leg?

2. Does he get out on a limb from which he cannot return?

3. Does he hide there and peek out on a situation, spying and sly?

4. Does he go there for privacy? To read a letter from some-one, perhaps?

Assignment

Choose one of these actions and write it down.

Now, follow along down this road—or up this tree!

1. *If* he falls out and breaks his leg—does someone come to help him?

    2. Does he lie there suffering and unconscious?

    3. Or does he crawl, deep in pain, toward a house for help?

Choose one of these actions and write it down.

    1. *If* someone comes to help him, is it a pretty woman?

    2. An old man?

    3. An old lady?

    4. The police?

Choose the pretty woman, for purposes of our illustration.

    1. *If* it's a young woman, does he let her help him?

    2. Or is he sullen and suffering and too proud?

    3. Does he know her?

    4. Or is she a stranger?

    5. Does he like women?

    6. Or is he a rejected child who has a quarrel with all females?

Choose one of these actions and write it. (If it isn't a pretty women, you could ask the same questions about whomever he's involved with.)

    1. *If* he has a quarrel with all ladies, does this pretty young woman change his mind?

    2. Or does he discover that she is just one more woman who has the power to anger him?

Choose one of these and write it.

    1. *If* she changes his mind, does he find himself growing to love her?

    2. Or does he fight like a wildcat for his independence and struggle against knowing her better?

Choose one of these and write it.

1. *If* he grows to love her, does he finally admit it?

2. Or does he hide it within himself, still afraid to trust?

Choose one of these and write it.

1. *If* he admits it, what is the reaction of the woman?

2. Is she free to accept his affection?

3. Does she love him, too?

4. Or is she married or otherwise involved so that she must turn him down?

Choose one of these and write it.

1. If she turns him down, does he go to the dogs?

2. Or is it an enriching experience that sends him into a new way of life?

You can see for yourself that this could go on for all eternity. There's also the most important question. Did he ever get to a hospital to have that leg set?

Now—taking your choices in order—write a narrative hook based on the first of the series of assignments.

Weave all the other choices together into as much copy as you can make from them.

(Who knows? You just *might* come up with a whole story!)

No matter how silly it sounds and no matter what fancy and obscure words are framed around the infinitive *to plot*—it's all here right under your nose. It's the constant matter of *choices*.

All of the elements of a complete short story are in these choices.

1. The *protagonist*—our hero—by moving up into that tree in the picture and in our imagination—gets himself into a predicament. This is the *problem* that all stories must have.

2. The way he responds to that predicament, and the complications which add up from that response, become the *plot*.

3. The way he solves that predicament is the "come-to-real-ize" or *resolution* of that plot.

4. Under it is the *theme*, the reason the hero is worth writing about at all.

That sounds simple, doesn't it? Then, why do we make so much of it?

DIFFERENT FROM LIFE

These choices (which really are a variety of predicaments) may be very involved, for one thing.

If you've lived any length of time at all, you know that each day *you* face constant decisions. The decision as to whether to get up or stay in bed; brush your teeth or ignore them; eat lunch or skip it; work or be lazy; go to class or cut it; walk or ride; stand or sit; speak or be silent; laugh or cry; love or hate. And thousands more.

Many of our own choices are made instinctively, without thought, and often without reason. Unfortunately—or perhaps fortunately—the characters we write about can't be so compulsive.

They have to have a good solid reason, an *understandable* reason, for every single move they make, every word they say, each thought they think, each emotion they feel.

This is called motivation, as we talked of back there with the case histories. Without the proper use of it no story will come whole and alive, even if you or your next-door neighbor are both without obvious motivation. Words on paper can be referred to again and again. All readers hate to be confused and see a character do something totally *out* of character.

Now—out of character is very simple to define. Test it yourself among the people you know well and care for Look at your spouse (if any!), your kids (if any!), your friends, your relatives. Knowing them as you do, interest yourself in imagining actions and dialogue which they'd probably rather die than do or say. You may come up with some pretty frightening ideas—or some amusing ones. It's all grist for your writer's mind, but don't write them, for pity's sake.

GETTING FORWARD WITH THE PLOT

There are certain ways for plots to proceed, over and above those choices that take you hither and yon. They, too, are selections you must make.

CHRONOLOGICAL

This means that you start at the beginning of the action and go step-by-step forward, in time lapse (or chronological) order. This is as steady and sure as day follows night. It could be called ABCD.

> To give you an example of ABCD in a story of mine in the *Saturday Evening Post* a little tomboy has grown up with a neighbor boy. Her father is dead but he has trained her to fish and hunt. Her mother, who wants to marry again, is in love with a quiet gentleman, totally unlike the girl's father.
>
> This was an ABCD kind of story. It began early in the morning and followed the girl through the day, through her trials with her mother, her mother's fiance and the boy next door, who suddenly seems to grow up as he tries to kiss her. The way the girl changes during this day to realize that softness and love are not so bad after all, is the context and the resolution of the story.

Straightforward and logical, this sort of story is good to write, easy to read, and can be managed if there are enough actual events—inside and outside of the protagonist—to give it a sense of continuity and action.

It is also a fine way to start any kind of nonfiction article.

Assignment

Select a day in your life.

Write a good narrative hook.

Try to get not only the actions of the day—but also your emotions, thoughts and problems.

Start in the morning and finish at night.

FLASHBACK

The second way to write a story is to start with a narrative hook of some power at a *high point*. This is a place where all action is at its peak, when the problem is most intense and unresolved.

When you get the reader really interested, then you can backtrack and tell what went before to *create* that point of action.

This gives you a chance to include description of background characters and past action. You've already lassoed your reader's interest with that high point.

When you've told the story in between, you come back to the beginning mix-up.

You solve it from there.

This is known as a *flashback*. You also could call it ABA.

For example, in a novelette in the late and lamented *Woman's Home Companion*, called *Beauty and the Dream*, a movie star was in a small motel in Santa Barbara. She was quiet and lonely there because the other customers stood in awe of her. She had come there because she wanted, for a week at least, to be like other people. She has a problem to solve. She also doesn't want to go back to her glamorous life, although she knows she has to.

This is the high point situation with which the story begins. It's the point of conflict where readers meet the heroine at a turning place in her life.

This is the point, too, where (to resolve her problem) she begins to remember her life and frankly goes back to redo it in that memory.

This is done with one flashback sentence.

"Her name was Marty Haller and she was sixteen."

When she has gone over it all, and readers know everything she knows about herself and her problem, she comes back to her present dilemma. The readers experience suspense because they have earlier knowledge of that dilemma and wait for her decision. They also know why she makes it, why it's valid for her because they know what went before.

Once again, this applies also to nonfiction.

Assignment

Start with a narrative hook that presents a problem.
Give your character's thoughts and emotions about that problem.

Then have him remember how the problem began in the first place.

Follow it logically until it comes back to the character's present dilemma.

Solve that predicament, based on his study of how it happened and what choices he has.

FLASHBACK IN FLASHBACK

When you get really adept, so that you can manage it without confusing your readers, you have a smaller flashback or two within the *main* flashback—which comes up ABACADA.

"The Day of the Decree" in *Today's Woman* accomplished this purpose.

Here, a young woman comes home, weary from work. She thinks a little about her present life, about the square dance she's going to with the man she is presently dating. And thinks about how they got to know each other.

When she opens her mail, she finds the legal document which means that her divorce is final. This takes her still further back. It tells another story about her marriage. It brings her again back to the present. It takes her to her relationship with the new man and how it may change now that her divorce is final.

The last return goes back to the beginning and resolves the way she truly feels about him.

Assignment

Give a character a present problem.

Have him faced in memory with a past problem.

Tell that story.

Return to the present problem.

Solve it.

You probably are beginning to realize now that all areas we have worked on apply to fiction and nonfiction alike.

A MATTER OF VIEWPOINT

There are still choices to be made before a story is going full steam.

The next thing is to decide from what viewpoint you want to tell the story and work out that plot.

If it's a short story, the almost inflexible rule (until very, and experimentally, recently) has been that the writer *must never switch viewpoint*.

This means that nothing can be seen, felt, comprehended, or described that isn't within the range of the single person viewpoint.

ME, MYSELF, AND I

You can have that single person be "I." This gives extra intimacy and identification. Or it can be "he" or "she." But, remember, whichever you choose, you may not go into the minds of other characters once you start.

Although this is a simple thing, it's also very important to your plotting.

I recently finished revising a novel, *The Long Terrible Day*, a suspense story.

When I first wrote it, it was in the third person—she—and the past tense. Much of it is in the mind of one woman.

This past year I read it over—it never sold—liked the basic idea better than ever—and began to work on it.

I went to the first person. "Sara Cochran" became "I." The change was immediate and satisfactory. It became a good and logical thing to have her think deeply, fear much, look backward and forward.

Then, to add to the feeling of danger and suspense, I put all that was presently happening into the present tense. I used the past only for her remembering. The entire quality of the work improved at once.

This, then, becomes an example of an entire full-length novel told from a single viewpoint. It limits, yes, but it also gives a certain personal involvement that can be effective.

Assignment

Find a short story written in the third (he or she) person.
Rewrite two pages of it in the first (I) person.

THE EYE OF GOD

Usually, in plotting longer stories, novels and novellas and novelettes, you can be a big powerful figure up above the words and people on the page. You can juggle everybody like puppets. You can see everything in one big paroramic sweep. You know all.

This is called the *omniscient recorder.* It's a sort of godlike state that allows all sorts of liberties.

The recorder does pretty much what the word means. He records the viewpoint of every character in the book. He's inside of each character, so that what they think and feel becomes clear to readers.

From chapter to chapter in a novel written by the recorder, you can be with the lives and feelings and thoughts of any number of different main characters. You can also be in the company of a sort of Greek chorus of minor figures. It's an exciting—if difficult—experience, living all of those lives. But it's well worth the extra effort of balancing and suffering over them. You become a very talented puppeteer, pulling wires on any number of characters on stage.

Assignment

Find a novel written in the first person.

Rewrite three pages of it to the omniscient recorder method. Put yourself in everybody's mind and give them each emotions and thoughts.

All right now, let's try a real experiment in plotting. I might as well admit it's sort of an experiment with me, too—as the complete "Not an Enemy in the World" is too long to be repeated in full here. Enough to say that it was published in *Alfred Hitchcock's Mystery Magazine*—and included in his anthology, 1981 edition.

And I'm going to try to summarize it—in part—by a series of paragraph narrative hooks.

> I always thought of myself as the sort of person of
> whom, if I were murdered, everybody would say
> "She didn't have an enemy in the world." . . . Af-

ter all, you spend your life really caring for people,
trying to get along with all of them . . . doing unto
others as they sure as hell never do unto you, and
you expect some understanding. . . . That's why
the letter came as such a shock. . . . I was in a hurry on my way to work. . . . Anyway I met the
mailman on the sidewalk outside my house. . . . I
double-timed it down to the corner. The bus was
just pulling away, but the driver knew me, so he
slammed on the brakes. . . . Well, I had enough
breath to say, "Thank you very much.". . . He
grunted without looking at me. . . . Seated, I
could see my nice, sleek desk. . . . If I could get
three letters out before Mr. Ingraham came in, I
could win one of his rare smiles. . . . I might just
as well admit it now as later. I'm in love with my
boss. . . . It gave me a purpose, a reason for getting up. . . . So when the bus came to my stop I
got off with a feeling of happy anticipation. . . . I
was alone in the elevator with the operator, Joe. .
. . I was always early, before the rest. . . . The
long corridor smelled clean and looked it. . . . My
key turned smoothly in the lock. . . . In the outer
office there were four desks. . . . Melissa, the
pretty, pretty thing, who always came to me for
help . . . George, the top salesman, whose desk
was most often empty. . . . On the right, at the
switchboard, Doris held sway. . . . At the desk
behind her, cornered away from the windows, was
Mr. Mealie who lived up to his name. . . . In my
more egotistic moments I thought Mr. Mealie was
in love with me. . . . Like almost all mornings I
stood looking at those desks with tenderness. They
were my life, my family, the four of them. George,
the smart brother; Doris, the naughty sister; Melissa, the baby sister; and Mr. Mealie? Well, an un-
cle maybe. . . . I kept my own office door locked
and nobody but Mr. Ingraham had the key. . . .
When I reached in my purse for it I pulled out the

stuff the mailman had handed me. . . . I sat down
on my comfortable chair and opened the first piece
of mail. . . . Subscription begging. . . . I put it in
the wastebasket. The electric bill. A letter from
Aunt Jane in a nursing home, which was thick and
would be whining, so I put it aside for my lunch
hour. The third was typed, addressed to me with
my middle initial, and had no return address on it.
. . . I opened it with a nail file. . . . I couldn't
seem to find my long, sharp letter opener shaped
like a sword with an etched handle, a gift from Mr.
Ingraham when he went to Spain. . . . My eyes
landed on the calendar. . . . There goes my lunch
hour. It was Leila Ingraham's birthday and I always shopped for her husband's gift. . . . Knowing his generosity I always bought the best, filmy
lovely things, which I dreamed I was wearing for
him. . . . I tore myself away from the dream. . . .
I looked down at the paper in my hand and read the
words quickly.

These words might have been in a foreign language so slow was my usually quick mind in a sort
of double take. . . . It was because of what the
note spelled out, of course.

"Dear, Dear Sara Ellison, Sweetie-Pie: "This is
to notify you that you won't have to wear out your
precious feet today searching for something expen-
sive and beautiful for Leila Ingraham and that your
boss will undoubtedly be late and highly disturbed
if he ever does come to work. . . . Because, you
stupid, adoring fool, by the time you get this,
Leila's broken body will have spent a dismal, chilly
night in the canyon below the Ingraham house.
Maybe even by the time you get this, it will have
been found and you will be accused of the crime. .
. . And Sweetie-Pie, it's some crime. You'd hardly
know her. That little Spanish letter opener, honed
razor sharp, does a real job. . . . That isn't the
point of this letter, really, although it was fun to

write the above and wonder what your sickly-sweet face looks like as you read it. If you're white and shaky now, dearie, hear this! You are going to be next! You'd better start looking over your shoulder as of right now. . . . It's none of your business why I killed Leila Ingraham, but you have a right to know why I'm going to kill you. I hate—most of all—women like you. Slobbering and catering to married men, always so damned sweet and cheerful and do-gooding. . . . So here you are. If they don't get you for the murder, with your fingerprints on that bloody, bloody opener, they'll find you sooner or later, dead as a doornail, a suicide from all that remorse."

That's it, then. That is not where the story stops, by any means. But it *is* where it ends. Because now you're ready—before you plan any projects of your own—for this assignment, which will find you plotting to the end.

Who killed Leila Ingraham? Who wants to kill Sara Ellison?

Assignment

Gather up your jigsaw pieces and try to fit as many of them as possible into an ending for "Not an Enemy in the World."

(This is an interesting thing to do with a full class as each writer comes in with a different and varied solution and it becomes eminently clear how uniquely writers approach the same idea, characters, situation and solution.)

Of course, different writers (even beginning ones) don't always stay within definitive lines. For some, an outline of plot seems likely. For others, a summary of the actions and movements. Some are even better off when they see the ending before they start.

But for now, learning step-by-step how to go forward in a story, it's often simpler just to take one careful, well-thought out step after another—letting the pages you wrote yesterday lead you into the material you'll cover today.

A recent student of mine was delighted practically all the time she was writing the book she has just finished.

"Every week, I wonder if I can keep on doing it," she told us.

"And every week another chapter comes out. It's exciting. I really don't know what's going to happen until I find myself making it happen. And I'm happy and pleased when it keeps on happening."

You won't always write this way. But for now it's a good place to be, a spirited manner in which to keep going.

With all of that behind you now, do you see how it can be with writers who get up in the morning with the glory in them of wanting to express themselves? Writers who have their characters, their reasons for a story, their good beginnings—and yet, who sit there and sit there—and then take to the sharpening pencil routine? Sometimes they even murder their writing because they won't keep at those choices until they come to the right, the needed, the perfect one.

They always can find it. So will you. You want to write. What you want to say is of some value. You have a sort of faith in yourself, as a human being, as a talent, as an observer of life and people. These are what keep you going in the long run: the day by day, month, and year searching for the series of plot selections that will be just right for the story you want to tell.

HOW TO STAY WITH IT

There are those who will inform you, I suppose, as you begin to write, that authors, like artists or actors or musicians, are a sort of hysterical and temperamental crew. In a way, they are. And for identical reasons.

Sticking to it is one of the biggest causes of nervousness. Keeping a thought in your mind on one page, while you know exactly what you want to say in plot the page after next, can be a shattering experience. Especially if you're interrupted.

It must be the same for an actor who almost knows his or her lines, or an artist who has just mixed the right color and is ready to use it, or a musician who has finally captured a difficult arpeggio—when the phone or doorbell rings. There's bound to be an explosion.

With the explosion, or the interruption, too many writers are apt to knock off for the day. So before we go any further, here a few tips on how to stay with that plotting once you have those sets of choices put into motion.

1. It's good psychology not to try to write when you know that you have little time to do it. Something about knowing that you have to stop to go somewhere in fifteen minutes or half an hour (or even for a professional a party at five) nudges the back of your mind and never allows it really to dig in unfathomable depth. Too, there's always the chance that once started, you may get inspired and want to keep going all evening and far into the night.

2. If, however, you can't work consistenly and for any great length of time, plan your plot in small scenes. Pretend that you're a motion picture director. Remember how it is with TV shows that fade in and out and go from place to place at the same time they're following one straight plot line. When you have one scene complete in your mind, write it down, even if you only have that fifteen minutes.

3. Be sure, whenever it's possible, of your *ending* before you start. This will help keep you plotting. Not the exact phrase, understand, although that may come to you sometimes. But if you know the *point* of the whole plot, you'll be able to continue with more consistency. If each step is unsure, whether you're heading east, west, north, or south, there's going to be a lot of backtracking and hemming and hawing, on paper and in your poor muddled mind.

4. If you know that you must be interrupted, when the time nears, *start a new paragraph* before you leave the work. It's amazing how much easier it is to pick up in the middle of something than at the end of something else. Even a sentence.

This especially applies to longer works. In a novel when you hit the end of a chapter and you're weary, it seems wonderful to have it finished, wound up, expressed to the best of your present ability. But many a book has turned yellow around the edges of the sheets because a chapter was done and the next one refused to come, for days, weeks, months, or ever.

So while you're rolling, put in that new sheet, follow through that idea which ended the previous writing, and get a page or so of the next thoughts down.

5. Cultivate a love affair with your subconscious mind. You'll not only fall in love with that mind, you'll respect and sometimes revere it. When you're stuck, stand up, stretch, relax, go for a walk, get a breath of fresh air, take a ride, have a cup of coffee, talk to someone about nothing. Think only about the activities and not of the writing

that waits for you back at the desk.

The results are practically always the same. When you return, still not thinking with your conscious mind, your fingers begin to fly. The secret, respected subconscious has solved the problem and taken the next step without benefit of you, or of seeming to think at all.

There's also something else you can cultivate—not only in writing, but with almost any problem. It may seem nebulous, but it often works. As you relax in bed at night, plant your story's snarl in your mind and doze off with it. Often your dreams will have the answer.

6. Trying to plug along despite all sorts of high water, there is always the quiet time in the dark, stretched out and comfortable in bed. There are the dreams, yes. But you can also learn to be a summer-upper. Go over, slowly and carefully, what you've managed to accomplish in the day behind you—on paper especially. Learn to be an anticipator. Plan the next step in the piece of work you're involved in. Once again, it's a weird experience, but your going-to-sleep conscious thoughts will be picked up by the subconscious as you sleep.

This is *not* dreaming.

It can keep you awake. But maybe you're sleeping too much, anyhow. You can get a sort of rest and assurance by knowing you have a definite, planned task awaiting you in the morning. Eventually, this combination of thinking will put you contentedly to sleep.

When morning comes you have something to go to as surely as a job where you punch a time clock. Only it can be far more exciting, because it is writing.

CHAPTER 11

The Fictional Summing Up

If you major in journalism or creative writing or even any other subject taught in high school or college, there's something you do several times a year—and do totally after your four-year course is taken. It's a frightening event and it takes a lot of cramming sometimes, much notetaking to help you memorize, and a good deal of organizing your thoughts.

This treacherous exercise is known, quite simply and powerfully, as the *final exam!*

So much depends on it in the average world that you create a good deal of tension in yourself, and sometimes in the life of those around you. We're not really a part of all that in this book, of course. Just the same, we need a sort of review—a coordinating, a remembering, before we step sharply into the area of fresh ideas, typing paper, and typewriter.

And so, we have now a final exam of sorts—or perhaps, if it makes you feel any better—a final assignment before we explore any other kind of setting words to paper.

First, buy yourself a fresh little notebook—or add pages to your loose-leaf.

Then take a look at the short story below. Read it for whatever enjoyment it gives you. Then, look at the identification questions at its end.

Read the questions one at a time. Scan the story for the answers—and copy that part of the story which demonstrates the use of the question.

Example: Mabel looked at the sick child and her heart thudded, her stomach in turmoil, as she reached to pick it up.

This would be a quote you would write for the identification of empathy. Ready? Here goes.

> I saw her first. Of course, in my business that's a phrase you hear a lot. What else you got to go on? You uncover something special. Then you beg, plot, and humiliate yourself in order to bring it into the light.
>
> Now that she's up there where the wind blows free and the spots shine hot and bright, half a dozen want to get into the act of discovery—the jockey who played "Jelly Beans" for the first time; the studio where they waxed it for seven bucks fifty; Music City where they took a chance and ordered in a thousand platters; the columnist who first wrote, "Listen hard to Janie Brooks. This one is going to orbit." You name 'em and toss a diamond needle into the air, you'll hit one of them.
>
> But I saw her first. There's this little hot dog place three doors from my office. When I've got a client worthy of the name I take him to the Huckster's, and we lay into a couple of martinis and a shrimp Louie. Mostly, though, I don't have clients worthy of the name. So I'm a familiar face in Dogville.
>
> Seven, eight months ago it was. I sat in my cubicle from nine-thirty till quarter of twelve. Nobody beat a golden fist on the door. So I read *Variety*, *Billboard*, and the *Hollywood Reporter* from cover to cover until it was time, respectably, to get outside and fill the gaspers with the burning-paper smell and the smog, and get me to Dogville.
>
> She was behind the counter and around it and beside my back booth as skittishly as a filly trying to prove itself the first clock at the track. She had a

curly mouth—that's the only phrase for it. She had a curly nose, too, which sounds crazy. It turned up to go with her smile and was splattered with pale freckles.

Her hair was black, her eyes were brown-to-black and her eyebrows were black, unplucked and strong as an Irishman's. There was a body attached, thin and little and strong, too. The whole ensemble I took in with a long look. It made her laugh. What kind of a laugh is it that seems to go up and down the scale, syncopated and full like a trained mezzo?

I said the thing that struck me. "You got a work permit?"

She turned the laugh off but her mough stayed curled. "Are you a checker?"

Looka here now, I thought, *the kid's a contralto at fourteen.* I shook my head.

"I was nineteen, for your information, on October twenty-fourth last. I do have a work permit. I've used it for over a year. The chili is especially good today." She leaned a little toward me.

I'm thirty-two years old and don't feel a day over ninety. This was a kid. But I backed away from her because what she was hit me in the face and the heart. I didn't want any part of it. And you can't stay young forever, can you?

"I put some extra onions in it myself," she whispered conspiratorially.

How can a whisper have echoes? All right, so if I'd actually discovered her, I would have added the whisper, the laugh, the talk, made a record, had it big. I didn't say I discovered her. I said I saw her first.

I ate my chili and stared out of the window. You see things in Hollywood you don't see anywhere else—not stars, except the ones they've painted white on the streets. Movie stars stay at home and catch up on a little rest, mostly.

No, what you see on the Boulevard is a lot more interesting. You see the ones who thought they'd make it and never got it and still pretend. For instance, while I chewed on an extra piece of the kid's onion one of them went by.

Corseted despite the heat, high false young bust, yellow wig doubled over on itself in that reverse kind of pompadour a cheap wig has, and flowing free in Mary Pickford curls all the way down the age-humped back, she limped along, her face runneled and painted.

Five steps behind her, like tomorrow stepping on the heels of yesterday, was a real hippy—beard, dirty T-shirt, dungarees low to the point of indecency, his sandals slapping the hot pavement.

You'd think I would get with it, being in the dead center of it all for so many years. But there's something in me from my ancestors that has a lot more in common with clean, well-dressed tourists.

I couldn't finish the chili. Somehow the old and the way-out young had managed to push aside the only good thing to come my direction in a year— that filly's smile and the chromatic laugh.

She was there again beside me and she was trying—I could feel it, like vibrations.

"Relax, kid," I said, not looking up. "What are you waiting for? A talent scout?"

She slipped the little roll of tape in front of me at the same time she snatched away the bowl of chili. "I'm waiting for you, Mr. Randall."

I looked up then. All right, so some of them still are vulnerable. Some of them have eyes that can open their doors and let you peek way back in, like a row of mirrors.

"What's this?" I sounded like I never saw a tape before. "How do you know my name?"

"Dolores, she works here, you know Dolores." I knew Dolores, all right. "And she said I could substitute next time she was out of town."

Back when I was getting educated there was a word for Dolores' out-of-town trips—"euphemism," it was called.

"Why?" I asked.

"Because I walked by your building—and I couldn't get the courage, and you come here. I need you, Mr. Randall. All I need is you—a manager, a good manager."

I sighed. I closed my eyes. They burned despite the air conditioning. All morning in my cubicle—staring at those newspapers, and nobody knocking on the door—and here she was, sounding as if I'd come from a plush office of my own building, with a gold sign on the outside, Richard Randall, Artists' Representative.

"Dolores says you're the best in the business."

Get that, will you? Two cheap dinners, one movie, three kisses and Dolores promotes me to head of the William Morris Agency.

I opened my eyes. There was a mirror at the end of the aisle of booths. I looked at us. I could see the circles under my eyes from that distance yet. The kid looked twelve, not fourteen, leaning over, eager, even her hair bent forward and asking.

"Give me the check," I said. "I'm in a hurry."

Do it clean. Everybody connected with the industries knows what I mean. Movies, TV, records, dancing, dramatics, whatever—do it clean. Cut it off sharp and tight to the nerve and get it over with and send them back home where they came from, where they belong.

The check was there. I fumbled for eighty-five cents plus tax, added a dime and slid out.

Way I felt, if I'd had a place I came from, I would have been on my way that minute. But at the door her hand came down on my arm. I wear short-sleeved shirts. She really touched me. I jumped and shook my wrist.

"I didn't hear you behind me," I said. "You got

no right to spook me like that."

"Here," she said quietly. She opened my hand and put the tape in it. She closed my fingers back on it. I stood there like a six-foot dummy in the waxworks, and she went back behind the counter.

"Too many onions in that darned chili," I found myself yelling. I slammed the door behind me.

My cubicle was hot. I turned the fan outward. Somebody said that helped. I sat down at the secondhand desk. If there had been room I would have set my feet up and leaned back and gone to sleep. I like sleep. It's dark there, and nobody's trying; and there's no charge, and the bills are paid.

Instead I sat bolt upright. Against the walls were all the pictures of the other ones. I started at the top line and studied them horizontally. A couple I got auditions for and talked up a great future for. Somebody listened—and it was all over.

They'd knocked at my door—last resort for most of them. I built them up and told them they had talent and got myself enough dough to go to Dogville and sleep in Mrs. Desmoines' back room. Why I ever put their pictures on the wall I'll never know.

There they were, fresher than springtime, newer than love, and all their young eyes reproached me. Never for a moment did those eyes admit that they couldn't sing or dance or act, that they could only exist and be young just once and that they would throw that youth away trying.

I turned away from them. In the corner was the hi-fi. There was the tape in my hand. I hooked it on—had to put it some place before it melted in my palm. On the way back to my pocket, my hand bumped against the switch.

And there was "Jelly Beans." And there was Janie Brooks. And there was I.

All right, all right—so she discovered me. She lay in wait for me and opened the fingers of my hand and set herself, in tape, on my palm. She said, in essence, "Here I am. I know I am here. Now you know. And it is up to you to tell them all."

The tape was made on a home machine. It had only a piano against that voice, a chord here and there. After three, I didn't hear them. All I heard was Janie.

OK, so maybe you don't like rock 'n' roll and think it's for kids and fools. That's the way Dan Elliot felt—and perhaps a million others. But it isn't time for Dan Elliot yet. It's just time to think about Janie—and "Jelly Beans."

Only I don't know how to say it, and nobody does. It comes along once in a decade, or a quarter century. When it lands it touches earth just long enough to skyrocket, or missile, or whatever. Then it takes off.

Art Tatum had it. James Dean had it. It was more than eyes or hands, or even talent. Rich— that was it; a richness of person behind all structure that cried out and said it for all of us, no matter what the means.

Janie Brooks had it in a silly little song about counting jelly beans in a jar, with just four basic chords hit at the proper time on the piano—and on a homemade tape.

When I got over it, which took longer than I would have believed, I ran back to Dogville. She was waiting at the end of the counter, leaning on her sharp little elbows, with her eyebrows black and strong, as if they typified her insides.

"Janie," I stormed while the door was still open.

"Jelly Beans," it had said on the tape. A Song by Janie Brooks, Accompanied by Jackie Brooks.

She lifted herself from her elbows and looked at me with all the doors open. I nodded.

"Yes," she said. There was never such a smile, not in Hollywood, California, there was never.

"Wait till I get my purse."

I was so excited I wasn't even ashamed to have her see my cubicle. She sat on the desk and swung her feet. I called people and grinned at her and all the young faces on the wall. It was like she'd vindicated the whole parade of them—and vindicated me, too, somehow.

When it happens in Smogville, it happens fast. Downstairs there was the recording studio, no bigger than a living room, but equipped with the right sort of stuff, precise as a watch. Across the street in Sam's Cafe there was the small combination of hopefuls, four of them stowing their hearts on the ends of horns and blowing them out in splinters— for peanuts and a chance at Larry Finley's show any time after midnight. In Janie's purse was the melody line for "Jelly Beans," badly copied because Janie didn't know much more than her small brother Jackie about notes on paper.

I corralled them all. I put Janie with them. Two hours later, after sitting in a dazzle of sweat and hope, watching them, yelling instructions, cutting them off, getting them started again, I knew we had a demo.

I picked up the platter as if it were already a gold one. I bought Janie a cup of coffee, gave her a couple of aspirin, took four myself, and sent her home. Then I started walking.

I wanted to give it to Dan Elliot. I knew that little disc in my pocket would make a place for itself anywhere in town—and anywhere in the country, eventually. But I wanted to give it to Dan. I had reasons.

It takes a certain kind of man to walk through the maze of this town and not get twisted around. Dan Elliot was that kind of man, even when I first knew him almost five years ago.

He walked into my cubicle one day back then and smiled and said, "Do you manage disc jock-

eys?" He put up a hand. It was a good hand, powerful and maybe it had used a shovel once, or held a
football. "A different kind of disc jockey," he
added. "One who wants good music and nothing
else."

I remember what I said. "I manage everybody
and everything. But there's no place in the business for a square deejay."

He had a "you poor fool, you" look on his face
then. "I said good, not square," he corrected.

I shook my head. He looked over the photo-
graphs carefully, sat down at the piano, sweetly
evoked a breath of Mozart, got up, put his hands in
his pockets and smiled at me. "You're adamant?"
he asked.

I nodded. "Man, I'm dug in," I stated deliberately.

So he gave me a thanks-anyway grin and walked
out.

The rest is history and it's holes in the head for
Richard Randall. That little gray building on Be-
verly I've been drooling over, that sports car, maybe a bachelor apartment, all of them could have
been mine—if I'd just had brains enough not to sit
there, dug in, and watch those straight shoulders
vanish through my cubicle door.

Because Dan Elliot had it. He got a job with the
smallest radio station in town. He sat on a kitchen
chair, boxed in by controls and tables, blond,
scrubbed, polite-voiced. From the beginning he
picked them—really fine packages, straight music,
honest sounds, new beats. He parlayed that station
out of the red with a broad, black stroke.

He parlayed himself too. That sure instinct led
him to Rose Recordings. First thing you knew,
there he was—president, no less. Romanoff's, La-
Rue's, every column and plug and cry boy around
wanted his seal of approval.

Only it was hard to get—especially with rock 'n'

roll. He wouldn't do many of them. Those he did went golden in a matter of weeks.

So I had to walk a long time, old "adamant" me. We never crossed swords or paths, and it wasn't going to be easy. But I wanted Dan Elliot for Janie Brooks.

I went down the Boulevard and over Gower. Finally I stood outside the modern building that houses Rose Recordings. I kept touching "Jelly Beans" there in my pocket. It was like touching Janie Brooks' black eyebrows, smoothing them. Strangely it soothed and strengthened me.

Man, but air conditioning, soft rugs, and gentle voices can do something to the metabolism of a thirty-two-year-old failure. It isn't magic either; it's misery. You get used to not making it, and the thought of success scares you silly.

Dan Elliot hadn't changed though. He put out his hand quickly and warmly. "What can I do for you, Mr. Randall?" he asked pleasantly.

"I've got Janie Brooks," I announced loudly. "And a song called 'Jelly Beans'; and I know how you feel about the jeans bit, but I'm doing you a favor—"

That was all wrong. I didn't have Janie Brooks. Just for a moment, her hand on my arm, and listening to "Jelly Beans" for the first time—that's all I had her. The excitement turned to lead in the chest. Just one of the crazy day's roller coaster rides. Second thing, nobody did Dan Elliot favors. Once he needed one, and who said no? What good is a favor five years late?

I took a deep breath against his smile. "Well, no," I corrected. "I'm asking one. I want you to listen to her. That's all. Just listen. First chance."

"I'll listen," he said quietly.

All the yammer went out of me. I watched Dan carry the little disc to the turntable. I watched the needle go down.

I closed my eyes at contact and I prayed—for Richard Randall, Artists' Representative; but mostly for Janie Brooks, who had stood beside my booth in an aura of faith and trying and wanting so strong it bit sharper than the chili with too many onions.

He never got back to his desk. The music of the boys from Sam's Cafe took one little lick. Dan took two steps. When Janie began counting jelly beans, he stopped so fast he could have had a gun jammed into his back—not a hair stirring, or a finger, until it was all the way through.

I knew how he felt. I shook with it, too, all over again. There was silence—heavy, like they say in books.

"Get her," Dan Elliot commanded, and he was a far cry from the kid I'd met that time. Top of Rose Recordings, he was, seeing the pennies flow free and beautiful, a copper Niagara Falls, into the coffers.

I bumped into two chairs and the corner of the desk getting to the phone. She answered on the first ring, and I could see her, little and dark and waiting. Her voice was her voice, and I had heard it always.

"OK?" she asked, "OK, Dick?" "Janie? Dick," I said.

"OK," I said. I wanted to bawl. "Come to Rose Recordings. It's a big man waiting for you." I turned toward Dan with the question on my face. He nodded. He looked gone and dreamy. "And a contract."

"Thank you." It's all right for nineteen-year-old girls to cry. It's fine for them to cry when it's happiness in their throats. "Thank you, Dick. Oh, thank you."

"For nothing," I said, sharper than I meant. "Now hop it." I let the receiver go down slowly and stared at it.

I'm not psychic. Who is? But I could see Janie

standing there beside Dan. He and Janie belonged together. They were two untouched in a touched community. They would make the rounds and the columns and get married and have wonderful, healthy, untouched kids. They'd both make a fortune and a fabled life.

"Sam's blow boys go with the package," I said firmly—businesslike; it takes hold easy.

Dan Elliot started moving then. He walked briskly to his desk, pushed buttons, shuffled papers and called a pretty secretary. I called Sam's Cafe.

It was a good moment—like Santa Claus in July—a very rich good moment when Janie walked in. And the hungry combo was on its way. If I twisted it just a little I could tell myself I did it all.

Janie's dress was red cotton with a small white pattern. She had brushed her hair smooth and pinned it up. She stood in the doorway and looked at Dan Elliot. He stood beside me and looked at her. All I had to do was wait awhile and see it work out.

"Build her up first," Dan Elliot told me. "Whet the curiosity. Plant the items. Get the interviews. We'll pick up the tab. I'll be busy here. Sam's boys can be the core, but I want a lot more—arrangement, solid in back of swinging jazz, strings maybe. And we have to do a flip side."

You start promoting somebody, you get to know him. I got to know Janie. She had a mother, father, brother Jackie. She lived in a house up one of Hollywood's side streets, and she was born there. Janie was sweet and wise for her years and glad about everything. She was breathless with Dan Elliot; and full of power, contralto, and sureness at the recording sessions. She had a million things to share with me.

Friend, it was a privilege. Every day I picked her up. We did the rounds of the deejays, local TV shows, newspapers. We left behind us a stream of words on taped interviews, notes jotted down for future columns, a fan club to be released with "Jelly Beans." Dan Elliot's name was part of the persuasion. Janie herself, with her curly mouth and freckles, was the other part.

I was just there, the carrier of the message, the chauffeur, the listener, the extra place at supper with her family, the one who taught Jackie the fifth and minor chord to go with his practical four.

It was enough. It was more than I'd ever had. It took care of the long hot days and the dinner hours.

Dan Elliot took care of the evenings—all of them. Janie looked strange and wonderful, very grown, in a sheath that glittered and a shimmering comb in her hair. She looked wonderful in print, in every column in town. She probably looked wonderful, too, dancing at the Crescendo, the Interlude, the Cloisters, Ciro's, The Palladium.

I didn't know about that, except what I read in the papers and clipped carefully and filed away in the folder labeled Janie Brooks.

But that didn't take care of the long hot nights— not by a bag of oats it didn't.

"Jelly Beans" was finally finished, with Dan Elliot's perfectionism. It was rock 'n' roll still. But it was something else, too, when he got through with it. It was "good music," and it would hold for a long time.

Dan took me into his office one day. "We'll take it from here, Randall," he said. He sounded good, but I wasn't sent by his voice. "Our publicity department has the after-release campaign all set up. Thanks for your help."

"Called off the case?" I asked.

He smiled. White teeth can look snow-cold; you ever noticed? "Janie," he said gently as always, "has a far place to go, Randall. Once she starts, you're going to be a mighty popular agent. You'll get your per cent for life. But we want to walk up there with her."

"You," I amended, almost under my breath.

"Me," he nodded. "Why not?"

OK, we stood eye to eye and toe to toe, like a couple of heavyweights. Then I shrugged. I predicted it, didn't I? I wanted to give Janie Brooks to Dan Elliot.

Janie called me once. "Dick." She sounded breathless. "Long time no see." That sounded phony. "I'm busy on the flip side." That sounded logical. "I'll see you at the party on the big night." That sounded doubtful.

I said yes to everything. OK, then, I got a cut into the contract; percentage, the gray building; soon as "Jelly Beans" hit, more clients than could drink martinis and eat shrimp Louie. I was Richard Randall, Artists' Representative assured.

I felt awful. I went to Dogville—the way you haunt the scene of the crime. I sat looking out of the window, and Hollywood was back in perspective—dreary, sad, going nowhere at all.

The *Examiner* said, "Dan Elliot is seen everywhere with his new find, the pixy Janie Brooks. Next week promises to weld them closer together than ever, when Rose Recordings releases the first shellac, "Jelly Beans.""

The *Hollywood Reporter* said, "Big fire blazing between disc exec Dan Elliot and one soon-not-to-be-unknown Janie Brooks, composer and vocalist who will next week be unwrapped by Rose." The rest were all the same.

I discovered that, by rearranging the filing case and record player, I could get my feet up. I found out that the fan turned in was just as stirring as turned outward. I sat in my cubicle and it was a matter of great pride that every time I picked up the phone to call Janie I put the receiver down before I dialed the number.

One day in the mail I got a package. I opened it, and it was the first waxing—"Jelly Beans," Janie Brooks, Sam's Four And Orchestra, it was labeled. I set it down very carefully on the player.

Then I got up and pounded down the hall and out into the street and across to Sam's Cafe, and I had two stiff, sudden drinks. Sam wasn't cordial. He hadn't found anybody else to play for peanuts and he blamed me.

I didn't mind. I didn't mind anything, except that it was release day; except that I had to go back to the cubicle and play "Jelly Beans." I had to.

I did. Afterwards I turned on the radio. On every station I hit, they were announcing it, had just played it, were playing it, or were talking about having played it. My phone started to ring. It kept on ringing most of the day—offers for Janie, dozens of them; even a few clients for Richard Randall.

By four-thirty I took the phone off the hook and totted everything up and copied it neatly. I let it get dark outside. I played "Jelly Beans" once more. At last I put the phone back on the hook and started to go. It rang again.

I picked it up. It was Janie. There wasn't a thing I could do. "Dick," she cried, "Dick, I'm on my way to the party. You'll be there?"

"No," I said. "What party?"

"Rose Recordings." There was a quiet. "Did you hear them? All day—"

"I heard them."

"You don't sound glad. Please be glad, Dick. Why won't you be there?"

"Janie," I said fiercely, "I'm tired. There's work on my desk. You're going so far up you'll never be able to look back." I stopped. I changed it. "Congratulations, doll. I'll get in touch. You and Dan have fun." I let silence run into the receiver.

Janie broke it gently in a voice smaller than I'd

heard before. "Did you play the flip side?"

"Flip?"

"The other side, dope." There was a little more tone.

"Not yet."

"Play it," she commanded strongly. She hung up.

I reached for the disc. I turned it over and snapped the switch. In the dark I sat down and stared out of the window. Hollywood was still there.

What was in my cubicle was pure and unfiltered, solid and terrible. It was Janie's voice, the whole of it, round and no beat, or hardly any beat—like a lullaby love song, so gentle, deep as a well.

Three words, over and over, were in between intimate little sentences of love. Three words—"I need you, I need you."

I don't care who you are, if you're ninety and dried ready to blow; or a cheat, or just Richard Randall, Artists' Representative. It isn't fair. It isn't right to listen to such a murmuring, such a secret delicious outpouring—not and know it's all for somebody else, it isn't.

No wonder she didn't want me around to hear her make it. I'm surprised she and Dan could let the control boys and the musicians in on it. "I need you." I guess I left the record spinning. I don't remember. I was just suddenly on the Boulevard. For once I didn't see any of them—neither the new trying ones nor the old pathetic ones.

I thought about Dan Elliot and Janie Brooks—a pretty picture, dancing somewhere, everybody coming over to congratulate them. Dan would stand up after a while and hold up those good successful hands for quiet.

"I have an announcement to make," he would say in that sure voice. "This is a big night in more ways than one—"

Mr. and Mrs. Dan Elliot. It figured. It fitted. I knew Dan had it for Janie the moment he saw her. I knew Janie had it for Dan, the breathless way she had with him. The flip side—how could you prove it deeper than that flip side?

Wherever I was, I turned around and started back to wherever I was going. I knew something for sure—I didn't discover Janie Brooks; I never had her. And I didn't want a gold-lettered sign. I didn't want to float to affluence on the hem of Janie's fluted petticoats. I didn't, as a matter of pure fact, want anything; not anything at all, from anybody at all in the whole stinking smog-filled world—except a cup of coffee. I'd take a cup of black coffee, bitter and harsh against my tongue. What do they call it? Counter-irritant?

I hurried to Dogville. I went directly to the back booth. Nobody was ever so tired. I put my elbows carefully on the table top. I made a cup of my hands, set my forehead into the cup and closed my eyes.

Through it all then, the weariness and—all right, let's go Hollywood dramatic—the despair, I began finally to feel it. It was a trying, like vibrations. "Relax kid," I said, not looking. "It's all right. Everything's all right."

"Of course," she agreed. She leaned forward. I felt the movement, the hiss of the party dress, the smell of new perfume. I kept my head down. "Did you play the flip side?" she whispered.

I sat up then, pulling on resources I hadn't ever used.

"I did, Janie," I said, quiet and dignified. "It's probably the most beautiful—piece of corn in the pops field."

You shouldn't slap a kid, honest. Not across the eyes. I made a smile. "Sorry, doll," I lightened it. "What I meant is—congratulations. You and Dan are sure to have the life perfect. And Dan was smart. That ballad opens up a whole new field—"

She nodded. "Dan and me. Yes."

"Wait till the deejays get hold of 'I Need You.' It's too good for a flip, doll. It should be the hot platter of the next hit."

She moved around the table and sat down across from me. "How do you know Dan is in love with me?"

"I'm psychic." I was, too—for sure, I was.

She nodded again. "Why didn't you come to the party?"

It hit me. "What are you doing here?"

I made her laugh. Her freckles seemed to dance. "Putting extra onions in the chili."

It was too much for me. "I have to go." I moved a little. Then her hand was on my arm, below the short sleeves, like that other time.

"Dick," she said, and oh, it was soft, just for the booth. "The flip side of 'Jelly Beans' is 'Lazy River.' "

"Huh?" I grunted.

" 'Lazy River.' "

"I don't get it."

"You will." she nodded. Her lower lip pushed out and up. "I—I made a very special cut, Dick; a one-of-a-kind master, Dick." I sat there and stared at her. She stared right back. Finally I got the strength to fish a dime out of my pocket for the coffee nobody had ever brought me. I stood up. She stood up, too.

We walked out of Dogville, faster and faster, until we came to the faded building with its echoing corridors. We went down them and into the cubicle.

The record was still spinning. In the dark I lifted the needle gently and set it down. I heard Janie's dress breathe and Janie breathe. I leaned against the wall. The record began. It went on. It finished.

With my head lifted I could see all those glossy photos dimly—fresher than springtime, younger than love.

So I kissed her. I kissed my girl. I kissed Janie Brooks. She kissed me back with her curly mouth, and I stroked her eyebrow—the left one, I guess. Yesterday stepped on the heels of tomorrow, and it was all now.

The tired old man of thirty-two was gone. The flip side was like all those up there on the wall, and I'd had it all the time. Only I forgot.

If you think you've heard Janie Brooks give out and over in any of the LPs or singles you've bought, you're dead wrong, man. You ain't heard nothing—not the golden record, the pure solid fourteen-carat polished and forever-golden record.

That's mine. Like Janie, that's mine for keeps and always. You see, I saw her first.

"Success Girl"—*Saturday Evening Post*

Final Assignment

Find examples of:
1. Universality
2. Sensitivity
3. Stubbornness
4. Faith
5. Observation
6. Total recall
7. Stream of consciousness
8. "I am the kind of person who"
9. Identification
10. Motivation
11. Physical description
     a. Sight
     b. Smell
     c. Sound
     d. Taste
     e. Touch
     f. Interweaving

12. Emotional-Mental description
13. Dialogue—Show where it
    a. Reveals information
    b. Forwards plot
    c. Shows location
    d. Reveals attitude
14. Identify theme
15. Narrative hook
16. Ask and answer reporter's questions
    a. Who?
    b. Where?
    c. What?
    d. How?
    e. Why?
17. Outline plot
18. Find flashbacks
19. What viewpoint is story written from?
20. Write a paragraph as to what appeals to you in this story.
21. If you feel that way—write about what you don't like.

CHAPTER 12

Fiction or Non?

One of these days, learning to write, practicing small exercises of various kinds to increase your facility and attain some craft, a strange thing is going to happen to you.

You're going to come smack-dab, face-to-face with a real idea. A universal idea. A marketable idea. A *good* idea. One that you never thought of before.

There was once an old expression when somebody cried, "I've got an idea!" It was answered, tauntingly, by "Treat it kindly. It's in a strange place."

It's more sensible than it sounds.

Nobody ever knows where ideas come from. You can stare for hours at a sheet of paper, trying to pull one reluctant fragment from some hidden source. And absolutely nothing will happen except that the paper gets whiter, more dazzling, and eventually defeats you.

You can be balancing your checkbook, taking a shower, practicing football, washing dishes, baking a cake, when suddenly, from nowhere at all a thought, total, beginning, middle and end, will walk into your mind.

It *is*, it always is, in a strange place. This is because it *comes* from a strange, unknown place. Both of which are to be respected.

It's the first part of that flip saying that concerns us now, though. That "treat it kindly" command that will be the yardstick to measure how far and how straight a path you'll travel on that terrible and thrilling journey from the dark of your mind to the light of the page.

It's so easy to be enchanted and excited with your great idea from nowhere. It's a simple thing to be carried away by the ease of conception, so that the birth is premature, unfinished, weak. It's much harder to hold back and restrain, to take care, to think over, to place.

Above all, to *decide*.

Decide what?

What are you going to do with that great idea now that you own it? Or, more aptly, now that it owns you?

You can ask yourself all sorts of secondary questions. Shall it be a novel? A play? A biography or autobiography? A narrative poem? An essay? A novella or novellette? A short story? An article?

These are minor questions and answers compared to the one Big Decision.

Shall it be fiction? Shall it be nonfiction?

Excluding poetry, if we think about it, everything we have read falls into one of these two categories. If you want to quibble about it, you can tie poetry onto the tail of this thought, too.

WHAT'S THE DIFFERENCE?

In making this important choice it's vital to know exactly what each area includes.

What is fiction?

According to our omnipresent referee, Webster, it means: 1) A feigning or imagining, as, by a fiction of the mind; 2) That which is feigned or imagined, especially, a feigned or invented story; 3) Fictitious literature, specifically novels; 4) Law. An assumption of a possible thing as a fact, irrespective of the question of its truth.

We have concentrated so far on that dimension.

To put a "non" before these definitions, of course, reverses them. So that *nothing* is feigned or imagined or really invented; nothing assumed, and all facts beyond question and true.

If you stick to the harsh lines of the "non" it looks, on the surface, as if you could write nothing in the world *except* fiction. In the broadest sense, though, no matter how factual a piece of work is, you always slant it to your own personal beliefs and color it with your attitudes and emotions.

However, by extending Webster into a wider concept, you come up with that simple choice: strictly imaginary pieces, whose only semblance to truth comes from things buried within your subconscious that slip out without your knowing. Factual writing about actual happenings or people or situations often requires research into the area of the nonfiction. The *New York Times*, for instance, always has squibs asking for letters, information, unusual facts about various people. The library, a newspaper morgue and actual interviews also contribute.

Let's try to trace this specifically.

1. To write an *autobiography* is to stick to real people and real facts as you write about yourself. As is a *biography*, only you're writing about the life of another person.

2. To make a *novel* of that autobiography is to be allowed all sorts of leeway, but to be impelled to cover, change, and merge all *true* descriptions and facts so that no one or no situation is recognizable as real.

3. To *fictionalize* the biography is to base it on an historical character or era, permitted only a minimum of imaginary license, and that only in areas where the minor characters, the minor life of the age, is unexplored and unresearched.

Beginning writers, naturally, are not about to jump into the sixty-five thousand word story of a life—theirs or anybody else's—or a full-fledged novel of any kind. To start with, despite the basic interest in words, it's quite enough to wring out seven pages and call it a short-short story. Or five pages and call it an article.

SHORT AND SWEET

It's this difficulty and this trying to make your new writing come out the proper length for its market, that gives both short stories and articles their value. That precision. You stay small. But you remember that both short stories and articles are fine springboards toward longer, tougher writing. One of them sharpens your imagination, the other gives you something to go on, a basic belief or framework for an outline.

Just as there is that jigsaw pattern in putting a story together, so is there one for articles.

In the past decade or so the reading public's interest has grown enormously in the field of the factual, semi-factual, how-to, or opinion type of writing. There are those who will claim that fiction, either by its quality or poor editing, has let the reader down. Especially in the magazines. We'll not debate that now.

Yet, it's well to remember that *more* books of all types are published today than ever before, and nonfiction books have increased a hundredfold, to compete strongly with novels.

But what forms does nonfiction take? The most common short form is the article—a prose composition, complete in itself, in a newspaper, magazine, or work of reference. Try reading the newspapers to distinguish news from articles. The article may express personal opinion, deduction, or evaluation and is usually bylined. The news tells *only* the facts of what happened.

Investigative reporting, by the way, is a good field, growing all the time. It covers a variety of subjects, often exposés and debatable issues—information about nuclear reactor construction and operation, for instance. Also all sorts of scandals, crimes in state prisons, mistreatment in mental institutions, nursing home atrocities.

City and regional magazines are following the national trend and featuring more of these kinds of pieces. All in all, it's a fine way to tackle nonfiction, either as an established writer or as a beginner.

But once you have made up your mind to work in the nonfiction area, you're faced with another question. What kind of article?

These are the general types.

STATISTICAL

This is a researched piece that has a definite point to make and sets out to prove it with figures and sometimes charts, graphs and artist's drawings. Like tabulated blocks, each point cannot be refuted and if piled precisely it becomes an overwhelming tower of proof. The increase in alcoholism might be an example.

HEALTH

This, also, is a researched article—into some area of the medical field this time. You've read them. Their primary purpose is to take the erudite and difficult and translate it into layman's language so that any reader can comprehend. A new drug on the market, perhaps, showing what it can do, where it comes from, what success it has had, what doctors and scientists think of its potential, the ramifications of its use—benefits weighed against side effects.

INSPIRATIONAL

A highly profitable and varied field, inspirational doesn't necessarily mean religious, though it's often included in the description. This kind of writing gives a little extra insight into some facet of life and uplifts the reader with its belief, optimism, and emotional appeal.

Examples would be how to deal with grief, or loss of faith, or any of today's trials and troubles.

PERSONAL EXPERIENCE

This tells of some event or experience of the writer that has general interest. It can either be universal (as, perhaps, how to get the most out of two weeks' vacation) or it can be touched with the bizarre or strange so that it attracts by its very uniqueness. A trip up the Nile in a kayak would do this.

PERSONALITY PROFILE

Here, you remember someone worthy of study or thought and tribute; an article on Schweitzer would serve this purpose. Or you might present an unusual side of a well-known personality—what a movie actress serves for a quick Saturday night dinner, for instance. This form often uses the face-to-face (or telephone) interview to gather material.

OPINION

All of us, especially these days and more especially those who try to write, have our own ideas on many subjects. Here's the place to express them. It always attracts reader attention when a writer gets on a soapbox about a controversial subject, and there are plenty of them. It's still better to take the unpopular side if you're up to it. It can be something as silly as "Why I Love Gorillas," or serious as "Why Learning Disabled Children Belong in Public Schools," or challenging as "Save the Ozone Before It's Too Late."

HOW-T0-DO-IT

This is one of the most popular of all and includes everything that you can do yourself, from building a house to making a thimble. To be successful, most of it should be based on the writer's own experiences. It must always tell carefully and exactly how to go about the process, what materials are used, in what amounts, almost like a blueprint. The many diet and exercise books are good examples.

HUMOROUS

If you're of that turn of mind, there is the humorous or satirical article. Most of these are about a familiar situation or group of characters, seen with a fresh eye and a laugh or a touch of ridicule. To read P.G. Wodehouse, Richard Armour, Mark Twain—even Robert Benchley—will give you the essence of this form.

If you look through any magazine, you'll find numerous subdivisions of these general rules: the nature piece, the food article, and other articles like these, and often sports and athletics. You can make your own list and choose whatever you are knowledgeable about or interested in.

Assignment

Write narrative hooks for

1. A statistical article

2. A health article

3. An inspirational article

4. A personal experience article

5. A personality profile

6. An opinion article

7. A how-to-do-it article

8. A humorous article

9. An essay

10. A treatise

It's most important, however, that before you write (remember, it isn't always just the words!) you have in mind the kind or type of article you want to devote your thought and time to.

Ahead of you are some pages devoted to the narrative hooks and beginnings of various types of articles. Read them carefully and then identify as best you can, which category they come under.

> Where worry is a mouse, a small scrabbling thing with sharp tiny feet, fear is a lion, with a roar and huge raking claws and teeth that can slash us to strips.
> Where worry, with work, can be swept from our minds, leaving them fairly clear, fear is a panic in the blood, an attacking of the heart, a complete blotting of normal thought.
> Fear is a thing all of us meet at some moment,

unexpectedly, like an animal springing from over-head and behind us.

There doesn't seem to be any way to avoid being occasionally, temporarily, even for just a moment, afraid when the unexpected happens.

But the thing that is happening to you, to me, to our homes, our streets, our towns and villages, our cities and counties, our country, our world, is the spread of fear like the spread of a plague.

Assignment

Identify which kind of article this is. Predict where you think it will go and what it is trying to prove.

I'll tell you who says it. The man who works eight hours a day, drives home, flops in a chair with a martini or a beer and stares at TV all evening. The man who won't lift a finger without time-and-a-half for overtime, double for Saturdays, and triple for Sundays. The man who plays golf all weekend, is too bushed to mow his own lawn and can't be bothered to crawl out of the sack in time to get to church service.

I'll tell you who says it. The woman who pushes a button to start her washing, has the great labor of lifting a load from the confines of the machine to the automatic dryer, and has darned little ironing because almost everything is wash-and-wear. The woman who spends her afternoon fussed up and girlish, at a bridge table, after a heavy morning of having her hair touched up in the beauty parlor. The woman who moans that all children are "such terrible problems" and, if she has to contribute to the PTA bake sale, spends five dollars for cookies from a fancy bakery rather than make them herself.

Assignment

All right now—what type of article do you think this is—and where do you think it's heading?

In the beginning of the next article a woman, who has not been feeling well, goes to her doctor, is told that she probably will have to have a hysterectomy, waits for tests and returns.

> "Well, Melinda," the doctor said and cleared his throat. He couldn't seem to think of anything else to add.
>
> "Well," I echoed. It sounded weak and girlish.
>
> He cleared his throat again, harshly this time, stated, suddenly loud and hearty, "You are going to have a baby."
>
> The enormity of it swept over me, after the doctor and my husband brought me from my faint.
>
> I was furious. What would my friends say? And Sally. How can I tell Sally she's going to have a baby brother twenty-one years younger than she—and a year younger than his nephew?

Assignment

There's a dilemma worthy of a piece of fiction, isn't it? But it isn't. It's an article. What kind? What does it intend to prove?

Assignment

Guess again.

> Somebody once said, "Don't give your heart to a dog to break." It is a sentence that rolls easily off the tongue, but it doesn't bear much thinking about. It is as if somebody had said, "Don't ever fall in love, or marry, or have children, or make friends—because something might happen to separate you from those you care for."

If you read these excerpts very carefully, thinking of yourself as sort of an "idea-detective," you can find that they are not one thing alone, but a combination of several types of articles woven together.

Assignment

The children line up around the room, with as much space as possible between them, and pretend to be clowns.

Teacher: "You are a clown. You are happy to be one. You are running. The hardest part is that you have to stay right in one spot—you have to look as if you were running a long way, but you keep your feet going up and down in the same place. Your arms go like pinwheels. Your legs lift almost to you chest with every step. You run and run. Now you begin to get tired. You slow down, but you still keep going. At last you are so tired you can hardly move, and finally you fall down exhausted."

What kind of article is that?

Consider this. As we mentioned above, no one of these types of articles has to fit tightly into one shape. Like all other areas of life and writing, the article is neither black nor white but is blended to a soft gray.

For example, in "The Loving and the Loved," an article of mine in *Cosmopolitan* a while ago, several of these types were interwoven.

"My mother had a stroke." This was *personal*.

"I believe that people should take care of their own whenever possible." This was *opinion*.

"My mother and I, working together, surmounted the many problems attendant on such a situation." This was *inspiration*.

I was asked by the editors to add facts about strokes, their background and frequency. I consulted doctors, and both *statistical* and *medical* slants went into the porridge.

The *personality profile* article became part of the whole as I remembered my mother and brought out her courage and patience and will to survive.

The *how-to-do-it* was really there as I told how she learned to eat and speak and move once again.

Only the humor was lacking. It wasn't an amusing situation, to say the least.

HOW TO PLAN AN ARTICLE

To keep an article moving, to make it readable and because you do not in the accepted sense have plot and action to play with, you learn the trick of *alternating*.

Good nonfiction will go from narrative to incident, then to anecdote, movement, dialogue, description, just as fiction does. You can use the flashback, the recorder, the first or third person, as you would choose to do in a story.

But you must, in order to hold interest, avoid that trap which so many new writers stumble into. That is the trap of just telling *about* your subject—all *narrative*. You have to make nonfiction happen, just as much as its more imaginative sister.

Articles, too, have an extra. At the end there is a *summation*. It should leave readers satisfied in the same way that the beginning intrigued them at the supermarket.

An outline here is a better idea by far than to outline the *plot* in a story. You have your material. You read over the general notes you have made of it. Then you carefully decide how you're going to make each point.

For instance:

A. Anecdote

B. Narrative

C. Description

D. Dialogue

E. Narrative

F. Incident

G. Narrative

H. Summation

You may vary this any way you like and have as many of each as you need. Note how you can keep going back to *narration* or telling *about*, so long as you break the copy up with the other forms that brighten it and point up what you're trying to say. This is what's called "open" copy, much easier to read and understand than dense, solid paragraphs.

HANDLE WITH CARE

There are as many ways to approach an article as a short story. The most interesting to read, and the most enjoyable to write in many ways, is the article with the fictional approach. With this approach you take advantage of description, flashback, dialogue, characters—whatever seems relevant, and works!

Here's an example from "The Loving and the Loved," again. I could easily have made it deeply personal, involved myself in a parade of our mutual virtues as we fought her way back to health, and come up with a "looky, looky, aren't we wonderful" type of thing. Quite obnoxious to any reader. Instead, I stood a little distance away from the two of us, and wrote it as if it were, in truth, a piece of fiction.

> One day Mrs. Jamison, aged seventy-six, a solid one-hundred-sixty, hair snow white and pin-curled, her room and life neatly organized, woke up feeling dizzy.

> After awhile, when the dizziness receded, she went into the kitchen of her daughter's home and fixed a small breakfast.

> She took it back to bed with her. "I'll just baby myself a little," she thought. She buoyed her shoulders with an extra pillow and began to sip her coffee and read the morning paper.

> By making my mother a character, by calling myself her daughter, Jane, I managed perspective on the pair of us, the things we'd shared together. I didn't get too emotionally involved, too lump-in-the-throat, in the telling.

Too much personal emotion, incidentally, is deadly to any kind of writing. It's quite easy to write some small thing that deeply touches you. You can finish it with a tear in your eye and the good feeling that it's a masterwork. You can send it out (or turn it in) and get a rejection in the speed of light.

When a comedian "breaks up" and laughs at himself, he somehow ceases to be funny. When a writer "cracks up" because he is so aware of emotion while he writes, he is no longer effectively emotional for the reader. You have to keep yourself one step removed. The best example of this is how it must be for doctors or nurses. No matter how tender, understanding, or sympathetic they may feel toward a patient, to get emotionally involved lessens their efficiency and hampers their success.

Assignment

Choose any of the types of articles listed for which you have written narrative hooks and write your choice in no less than five hundred words.

(Remember that only the humorous, opinion, personal, and inspirational need no research.)

Incidentally, *research* again, means just about what the word divided does. From sources where a search of the subject has already been made, you study them, collect them, and search into them more deeply or from another angle entirely.

Take the article you have written and, if possible, give it a fictional approach.

If not, start fresh with another idea and see what you come up with using this approach.

This is the great thing about a good idea. It is *durable*. It will serve you in more than one way, and in many different phases of writing.

It can be used as *both nonfiction and fiction*.

NOTHING NEW UNDER THE SUN

"They" say, as we mentioned, that there are really no original ideas left in the world. Don't argue the theory. Remember instead that all ideas depend on how they're used.

If you return momentarily to that individuality which you began searching for at the beginning of this book, an idea of mine *written by you*, would be an entirely different story than if I worked it out. And vice versa. We are different, our viewpoints are different, our backgrounds are different.

Let's then trace the development of an idea into *two* salable pieces of work.

1. In my idea book, I wrote "physical attraction." Certainly *not* original.

2. Eventually, there was the theme. This came from my work over the years with teenage girls, and their problems. One of these, explored time and again, was the wisdom or the foolishness of too-early marriages.

3. In a book, *Heaven in the Home*, I found myself starting with this theme. It was a logical place. The book was about all phases of marriage, children, and life in the home.

In the book, I treated physical attraction like this: Don't be trapped by touch, Cathy. So many marriages have failed because of that. We stand, as girls, yes, and as boys, too, with a sort of wind against us. Inside, there is the turmoil and the reaching. There is the knowledge that we are half of something, the inborn instinct to become whole, to get on with a total sort of living.

This is a God-given thing. It is a miracle. From it stem all of us, back to the beginning. So the wind is on us, and the drive is in us. Then somebody who looks fine and young and clean walks toward us. The touch is new. It is beyond anything we, untapped, remote within ourselves and waiting, have ever known.

Because we have read, heard, and thought of love with our growing, the quick exultant conviction comes to us that we have found it. Found it with that touch.

Happiness ever after.

Cathy, you're a big girl now. I can speak to you freely. You read the articles. There are so many of them. Articles about failing marriages. About how to hold your husband. About all sorts of sex adjustments and intricacies.

They are all based on touch.

4. It was nonfiction. I called it "The Cinderella Story." Before the book was published, *Family Circle* bought that chapter and print-

ed it under the title "Is He Your True Prince Charming?" This was an article.

    5. Later, another year, with the girls still in high school, they worried about losing touch with their boyfriends when they went away to college.

With the greatest of ease and no feeling of repetition, I found my way to "First Star," sold to *Seventeen*.

    This was *fiction*.

>   The first time they had ever kissed was in the park.
>
>   "I don't feel like it," he said now. It sounded loud. The whole street was suddenly quiet.
>
>   Cindy held her breath. To say that he didn't want to go to the park was the same as telling her he didn't want to kiss her. They always kissed in the park.
>
>   The tickle in her throat was a band now. Her words worked their way past it. "We could take a ride. We could park. And talk."
>
>   Parking was stronger than being outdoors. Headier. She didn't allow it often, hardly ever. The windows let in small gusts of evening air. Off on a hill somewhere, the lights uneasy below them, she got a shut-in, private, sort of married feeling. It was what Bob liked best, alone, high above the world, two. Loving.
>
>   If he said no—
>
>   He said it. "No, I don't want to park."
>
>   It was hard to swallow. "What then?" She sounded petulant again, as with her mother.
>
>   "We have to talk, Cindy."
>
>   "Why?"
>
>   She could get lost in Bob's words. She knew that well. He was Honor Roll. He was Senior Class president. He was smart and he knew a lot of things that she never understood. She didn't feel safe when Bob talked. She only felt safe when he held her, when he kissed her.

Assignment

Write an article of at least two hundred words. Keep in mind the second half of the assignment.

Adapt the article *theme* to a short-short story of not more than eight hundred words.

To practice then, in this field of articles, there are a few simple things you can do.

First, search through the maze of your beliefs, opinions, interests. Remember trips you've taken, people you've known and respected. Look with a clear eye on problems you, or your friends, have known and faced—or evaded. Examine some of the little shortcuts you've invented to help you work, your hobbies, the things you do with your hands.

Then write about them. You don't have to do great, long reams. Brevity makes them even better.

Some general things can be said about writing articles. In many ways, and for many writers they are much easier to do. They can be filled with opinions, beliefs, examples, facts from books, figures— much of your material is already there for you to assemble uniquely. This hardly ever applies to fiction.

In today's markets articles are easier to sell because all publishers use many more of them than fiction. In the book department, they're always fat on the bestseller lists. Think how very many books have been published in the last few years about diet and exercise and nutrition alone.

So, even if your first love is fiction, it's wise to keep a separate idea book of article seeds that may flower one day when you're suddenly struck with the right way to approach them.

Now that you have practiced writing articles to short stories, perhaps you'd like to know what type each article turned out to be. (Just to urge you on!)

1. Conquering fear, "The Face of Fear . . . Heaven on the Doorstep," inspirational.

2. Standing up for teenagers, "Who Says Teenagers Are Soft?" *McCalls*, double duty, personal and opinion.

3. Menopausal babies, "I'm Forty-Five Years Older Than My

Son," *Cosmopolitan*, combination: how-to, health, inspirational, and statistical.

4. How to enjoy a pet, "Let's See What He Does," *Popular Pets*, personal, inspirational, opinion, how-to.

5. How-to-do-it paragraph book of *Creative Dramatics*.

With every one you write you'll become more proficient in the whole art. When you've done a few of them, explore the themes carefully. See if perhaps you can't get double duty from that really good idea—when it hits you.

Because it will, never fear. You will then be ready for it. You'll have trained you mind, your fingers, and even your heart—to decide what to do with it when you get it.

You'll have learned how to "treat it kindly" in every sense of the word.

CHAPTER 13

The Nonfiction Summing Up and a Forward Look

Just as with fiction, if you're going to write from the inside out, you are wise to gather together everything you have learned—tangible and intangible—to be certain that you know and remember the simple, yet varied bits of practice you've been doing. Your mental jigsaw puzzle has to fit neatly, every piece in place, before you begin a project.

As with fiction, nonfiction can be analyzed and studied for the various dimensions of approach and continuity.

So—as after-dinner introductory speakers often say—here, without further ado, is an article. Read it slowly for its content and overall meaning first. Then go slow-motion and look for the points requested at its end.

> Where we live, on the Eastern Shore of Maryland, the gentle waters run in and out like fingers slimming at the tips. They curl into the smaller creeks and coves like tender palms.

The Canada geese know this, as do the fat white swan and the ducks who ride an inch above the waves of Chesapeake Bay as they skim their way into harbor. In the autumn, by the thousands, they come home for the winter.

In the hunting season the air is filled with the sound of guns. The shores are scattered with blinds, the creeks and rivers with duck and goose decoys. The swan are a different matter entirely. Protected by law, they move toward the shores in a stately glide, their tall heads proud and unafraid. They lower their long necks deep into the water, where their strong beaks dig through the river bottoms for food.

And there is, between the arrogant swan and the prolific geese an indifference, almost a disdain.

Once or twice each year, snow and sleet move into the area. When this happens, if the river is at its narrowest, or the creek shallow, there is a freeze that hardens the water to ice.

It was on such a morning near Oxford, Maryland, that a friend of mine set the breakfast table and poured the coffee beside the huge window that looked out from her home on the Tred Avon River. Across the river, beyond the dock, the snow laced the rim of the shore in white. For a moment she stood quietly, looking at what the night's storm had painted.

Suddenly she leaned forward and peered close to the frosted window. "It really is," she cried aloud. "There's a goose out there."

She reached to the bookcase and pulled out a pair of binoculars. Into their sights came the figure of a large Canada goose, very still, its wings folded tight to its sides, its feet frozen to the ice.

All day she watched the trapped goose, unable to reach it with pole or boat. Unable to walk on the ice because it was too thin.

Toward twilight from the dark sky, above the

setting sun, white against its lackluster, she saw a line of swans. They moved in their own singular formation, graceful, intrepid and free. They crossed from the west of the broad creek high above the house, moving steadily to the east.

As my friend watched, the leader swung to the right. Then the white string of birds became a white circle. It floated from the top of the sky downward. At last, as easy as feathers coming to earth, the circle landed on the ice.

My friend was on her feet now, with one unbelieving hand against her mouth. As the swans surrounded the frozen goose, she feared that what life he still maintained might be pecked out by those great swan bills.

Instead, amazingly instead, those bills began to work on the ice. The long necks were lifted and curved down again and again as deliberately as picks swung over the head of a fisherman cutting a free space for his winter rod. It went on for a long time.

At last the goose was rimmed by a narrow margin of ice instead of the entire creek. The swan rose again, following the leader, and hovered in that circle, awaiting the results of their labors.

The goose's head was lifted. Its body pulled. Then the goose was free and standing on the ice. He was moving his big webbed feet slowly. And the swan stood in the air over him, watching.

Then as if he had cried, "I cannot fly," four of the swan came down around him. Their powerful beaks scraped the goose's wing from bottom to top, scuttled under its wings and rode up its body, chipping off and melting the ice held in the feathers.

Slowly, as if testing, the goose spread its wings as far as they would go, brought them together, accordionlike, and spread them again.

When at last the wings reached their full, the four swan took off and joined the hovering group.

They resumed their eastward journey, in perfect, impersonal formation, to a secret destination.

Behind them, rising with incredible speed and joy, the goose moved into the sky. He followed them, flapping double-time, until he caught up, until he joined the last of the line, like a small dark child at the end of a crack-the-whip of older boys.

My friend watched them until they disappeared over the tips of the farthest trees. Only then, in the dusk which was suddenly deep, did she realize that tears were running down her cheeks and had been, for how long she didn't know.

This is a true story. It happened. I do not try to interpret it. I just think of it in the bad moments, and from it comes only one hopeful question: "If so for birds, why not for man?"

Assignment

1. What type of article is it?
2. Find passages that are fictionalized.
3. Identify passages that are autobiographical.
4. Where is it inspirational?
5. Where is it personal?
6. Where does it show character?
7. Where is there opinion?
8. Is there how-to-do-it? If so, where?
9. Find humor.
10. What's the theme?
11. What does it set out to prove?
12. What is the phrase that tells the reason for the whole article?
13. Find examples of sensitivity and universality.
14. Is there a moral? What is it?

Now, when you're sure of your answers, when you've identified and written them down—take another step.

Go back to the Final Assignment for fiction on page 139. Look over those questions carefully. Check your answers. See how many of them apply to both the fiction and nonfiction and label the points where they do so.

READY, SET, GO

Whatever area of writing—fiction or nonfiction—one thing, eventually, is bound to happen.

When a baby has learned to sit up and to crawl, he stands and takes his first step, clinging to strong older hands.

But eventually he walks alone.

When a child goes forth to his first day at kindergarten, he does so reluctantly, and sometimes in tears.

But in less than a week he's happily adjusted and hates to hear the ring of the closing bell.

When a young person leaves home for the far-flung world the first time, there's a strange sense of loss as the pattern is changed.

In all cases, young or older, there's a sort of leap into very deep waters indeed—and a sink or swim ultimatum.

That is the point which you have now reached in writing.

Realize this, please.

It's quite possible to continue through countless pages on all of the fine and often quibbling points of writing techniques of any and every form of fiction or nonfiction, in any and every length. Whole books can be devoted to playwriting, television, the art and analysis of poetry, the essay, and the short story. They have been. They are available for any tangential reading you may wish to do in a specific area.

There is one weakness, one fallacy in too much analysis, too much reading, though.

It can easily get to be a perpetual postponement.

The reading, the study, the understanding, and analysis can get to be a career in itself.

FREELANCE STUDENTS

All over the country and perhaps the world, there are writing classes in continuing education and seminars. There are would-be writers who fill them. They stay, eager as beavers, throughout the duration of the course—the learning period.

But all writing courses come to an end. Those freelance students disappear. To reappear in the magazines or with a novel? Or a book of inspiration, philosophy, or a play? Seldom—if ever.

Where they show up again is in another writing course. And another. They call themselves "writers" with more and more assurance each time.

But they are *not* writers. They are nomads with typewriters. The trip is their goal, not the destination, whether they realize it or not. They rarely can show a finished piece of work. They stay forever on one thing or switch from idea to idea as they switch from class to class. One man I know has been working on a novel for almost fifteen years. He still hasn't written "The End." So listen well, please!

When I was young, hanging over my bed was a print. It was pretty and feminine and went with the new bedspread my mother had bought me. It showed, in gentle pastels, a young girl with golden hair, in a pale pink dress, lifted just slightly above her dimpled knees, beside a rippling, very clear creek. She had one slim leg on land, the other dipping a toe into the bright water.

The girl looked happy. But she also looked a little timid and *very* cautious.

Underneath the picture in sort of ornate print, were the words, "Standing with reluctant feet.

Where the brook and river meet."

There was supposed to be significance to this, you understand. In my day, sex was a hidden sly animal in a deep dark cave. But such a charming picture could hint, very delicately, that little girls didn't stay little girls, and eventually their "reluctant feet" jumped right into the river. Hurray!

And so it is with you, right now—no matter the years hung upon you. No matter how little real reluctance you feel, now is the time when you begin to step out a little to see whether you are going to sink or swim or run away entirely.

If you've sincerely followed the assignments as we moved along, you have (among them, perhaps) all of the ingredients to put together a piece of fiction or nonfiction.

This is a good feeling, a fine thing to know. But it also can be most confusing.

START NOW!

Over the years you've wanted to write and haven't been able to get to it—waiting for the children to grow up and away to give you some time; waiting to grow old enough to take a serious course so that some of your youthful dreams and hopes could be expressed in words. Or, perhaps, even as you edge toward retirement, you're planning to set your experiences, practical or not, on paper. You've collected in your mind, an idea book of conversations or intimacies, dozens of ideas. Many of them are just bits of thoughts. A rare few seem to have life and body. But they're there, jammed into the Pandora's box of your subconscious.

As you learn methods for releasing the contents of the box, sort of like forging a key for it with studying, you have to be careful of two things.

1. Don't let them all jump out at you at one time. If you do, you'll be as besieged as by a runaway, angry, swarm of yellow jackets.

2. And don't let their number turn your thoughts into the sort of rider they talked about when they quoted, "He rode off in all directions."

So the question which faces you, of course, is *what* do you write? Remember that idea book? Remember total recall?

This is the time to bring the book out—and the time to carefully study a new variation of recall.

This is also the disappointing and somewhat sad time in a writing course. Especially a large one. Strange, but so long as the lectures continue, the assignments are given precisely, the students, young or old, in school or in evening classes, maintain a good bit of enthusiasm and show considerable talent. But let the time come—the assignment happen—where they're asked to create a project for themselves and the faces droop, the written pages grow thinner. In adult classes whole bodies disappear ("because I didn't have anything to bring") and in school the grades drop with slim sentences haphazardly written.

These are the ones who are "playing at being writers," who haven't taken careful notes, or practiced each assignment with diligence. And of course, of *course*, it doesn't apply to any of you who are reading this book!

After all, you have stayed with it to this far page. You may have had a few difficult moments—but you have produced, not only specific assignments, but much of what is the original and unique *you*. Sure, you're a little reluctant. You're testing *yourself* now. But you don't have to be timid. Pull out the idea book. Study it carefully.

Find the one idea that perhaps has haunted you the longest or excited you the most.

You write half a dozen narrative hooks and choose the one you prefer. Then you sit back and dream a little. You do a thing that isn't quite total recall—let's just call it looking backward.

Sometimes it seems life is like a train with many cars. They carry the various passengers (yourself at different ages), so that years from now you can walk through them and speak to strangers, recognizing only their faces or the way they move their hands or inflections of their voices as yourself at a certain age and stage. All the same train. But what varied coaches, strung together from so many different obsolete railroad lines, no resemblance to each other except that the same older self will one day walk back through them.

This is the idea. The thought, too, that will set you to the project—in time and space.

You have to decide, when you start to write for yourself, what period in your own life is going to come clear enough so that you can duplicate that period—and perhaps the emotions, thoughts, characters, and background that were familiar to you and bring them into focus for your reader.

Then you are ready to write! And you make yourself a firm promise. Whatever you start, you are going to finish!

FLYING SOLO

The moment of truth is here. The baby takes that first step alone. The child makes his own way in school. The young person runs his own life and stands or falls by his own decisions. And—given enough time—the professional writing student runs out of courses—and even of books.

An old saw, tossed around for generations is, "The best way to learn to write is to *write!*"

It isn't totally true, as are many old saws. You can beat your brains and heart out doing anything the hard way, without preparation, help or teaching.

But that old saying has its validity.

So here you are now. You're between the person who knows nothing of writing and tries—and the one who goes on and on, studying without doing.

It's a good position if you deal with it properly. Ideal. You're ready—and you're ready in fine proportion.

Choose your own project. Begin it. Work on it. Finish it. You know how to take each step because you've taken them. When you're caught or confused in one area, you refer to the chapter that it concerns and apply the practice assignments to the problem in your project.

Don't allow yourself too many starts. Sometimes it seems good to juggle a couple of projects—refreshing in both areas—such as an essay or article or a piece of fiction, working on one when the other dries up. But scatterbrained is scatterbrained. So take care.

This is the time now, too, to read what others have done in the field of your particular project. It's rewarding not only because you can, in light of the knowledge you've acquired, perceive the craft, the skill, and the variety each author has used. You can also be a critic of sorts. You see what weaknesses or flaws they may have. This can be heartening. You know that all are not perfect. Maybe, in some cases, you could do as well.

Here are some definite terms (which you probably know) and some recommendations for reading to go with them.

SHORT-SHORT STORY
This is a story that runs around fifteen hundred words.
It usually, though not always, has a surprise twist of some sort at the end. It is *not* just a little character sketch. It has a beginning, middle, and end.
Read: O. Henry's "Gift of the Magi."
In today's market, the only places that short-shorts can be seen regularly are *Redbook*, *Good Housekeeping*, *Ladies' Home Journal*, sometimes *The New Yorker*, and the little magazines.

SHORT STORY
This is a story of no longer than four thousand words, as a rule.
Read: *How We Live*, an anthology of contemporary life in contemporary fiction, collected by Penney Chapin Hills and L. Rust Hills.
Nine Stories, by J.D. Salinger
The Short Stories of Ernest Hemingway

Also, watch the *Atlantic Monthly* or *Ellery Queen's Mystery Magazine* for their First Appearance stories.

NOVELETTE
A very short novel—or a very long short story, usually in popular magazine style—fifteen to twenty thousand words.
Read: Any "back of the book" suspense stories in *Alfred Hitchcock's Mystery Magazine*.

NOVELLA
A short novel of around thirty-five thousand words.
Read: *The Red Pony*, by John Steinbeck
Old Man and the Sea, by Ernest Hemingway

NOVEL
A fictitious tale or romance—around sixty-five thousand words, though many run much longer. (A new market here is Avon Books, which is looking for first novels.)
Novels come in many guises, of course. Although it's rather hard to pin them all down—to set any one into the limits of a definite category—you might consider these.

1. Family saga
   Thorn Birds, by Colleen McCullough
   Dinner at the Homesick Restaurant, by Anne Tyler

2. Love story
   Sophie's Choice, by William Styron
   Love Story, by Erich Segal

3. Historical
   The Bastard, by John Jakes
   Lust for Life, by Irving Stone

4. Mystery/suspense
   any John D. MacDonald novel

5. Horror
   Cujo and *Christine*, by Stephen King

Make your own list. Then, as you read, or when you've fin-

ished reading one, figure out for yourself what type of novel it is. It will give you sort of a rough pattern to fit your work into—when you do it!
Read: *To Kill a Mockingbird*, by Harper Lee
The Wall, by John Hersey
Look Homeward, Angel, by Thomas Wolfe

ESSAY
A short written composition—an experiment, usually in thinking and opinion.
Read: The essays of Ralph Waldo Emerson

TREATISE
A written composition on some particular subject, in which its principles are discussed or explained.
Read: *Essays of the Masters*, edited by Charles Neider, which contains both essays and treatises.

AUTOBIOGRAPHY
A biography, account, or character sketch of a person written by himself.
Read: *Speak Memory*, by Vladimir Nabokov
The Autobiography of Benjamin Franklin
Growing Up, by Russell Baker.
You do not have to be really old to write an autobiography. With your search for total recall, back into whatever years were younger for you, you can find a picture of childhood or adolescence that can talk to many readers.

BIOGRAPHY
The true story of the life of a real and particular person. the length varies; usually not less than sixty-five thousand words.
Read: *Madame Sara*, by Cornelia Otis Skinner
Thomas Wolfe, by Elizabeth Nowell
Papa Hemingway, by A.E. Hotchner

FICTIONALIZED BIOGRAPHY
The story of a person's life, taking the liberty of surround-

ing that person with events and people created by the writer, and endowing him with characteristics, thoughts, and emotions which couldn't really be known.

Read: *The Confessions of Nat Turner*, by William Styron
The Agony and the Ecstasy, by Irving Stone

When you read, read to enjoy yourself. But also consider what we have learned here—read with an eye for the unusual turn of phrase, the brilliant piece of dialogue, the subtle description, the deep character.

You'll find that reading this way will enhance you, not only as the average reader, but will add to what you have tried to put into words yourself, and will help you to do so more freely from now on.

CHAPTER 14

Cut, Revise, Rewrite, and Polish

When you have finished a story, or an article, you'll find yourself on top of the world more often than not. This is due to the simple fact that you've managed to *start* a piece of work—to *keep it going* from paragraph to paragraph—and to *finish it.*

It's probably the happiest and most light-hearted moment of a writer's life. To use our baby analogy—the child is delivered, and it looks beautiful to you, just because you don't have to carry its heavy struggling weight any longer and the pain of delivery is over.

One thing is true, though. You're apt to see that baby with a prejudiced parental fondness that the clear impersonal eyes of a professor or an editor don't share. *If* you copy it in a big rush and hand it right in, you can maintain the illusion that it is a lovely thing. Your optimism persuades you that he'll undoubtedly think so, too.

The first criticism or rejection can easily disabuse you of this notion, as we mentioned way back there. It tosses you to the other end of the pendulum. Out on a limb. Sorry for yourself. Even hating the piece of work. Disliking the new baby more than it deserves.

In other words, with one harshness you question your ability to write at all, being a "sensitive soul." It doesn't matter whether you're a brand new writer or an old salt, those criticisms sting.

STRIVE TO BE OBJECTIVE

Consider this. You will *always* get and have to deal with those rejections and criticisms pointed out clearly in the discussion of writers' hazards. Even a good attitude toward them doesn't solve the problem.

But some rejections, and many of them if you write a good deal, are *absolutely unnecessary.*

You get them because your piece of work wasn't really *finished* in the full sense of the word when you turned it in. Like a premature baby.

When that article or story is back home and time has passed, you'll find that you can pick it up and *remove yourself* from it as you never could have done when it was fresh and new and treasured. You can sit down, forgetting that you're supposed to be a writer, and be what you have been as a lover of words all your years. You can be the *average reader.*

This is not exactly easy, but it's nowhere near as hard as it sounds.

You *read* through the piece. You *decide,* if it were in a magazine and you were in no way connected with it, whether or not you would *begin* to read it in the first place, *stay with* it in the second place—and get *anything at all* out of it in the third place.

Assignment

Here are three examples. Read them carefully. Then answer the questions.

1. In the mornings, that summer when he was nine, stretching out in bed, with the hot sun slamming behind the curtains and breathing on top of his head, Joe felt the length of himself reaching farther than it ever had before.

2. It was the night before, in the kitchen, Monna turned ham, slipped the spatula under the frying potatoes, flipped them on their backs, exposed their golden fronts.

The smile on Bunny's face was a thing she could feel, as if her cheeks made apples of themselves below her eyes.

3. It happened every year since the time of Donny McBane's first remembrance. Somewhere between Christmas and Easter the feeling would come on him, and he knew, in the marrow of a bone or the alarm clock in his wintered muscles, that it was time to build a kite.

These are all stories about children, as you can see. You are *truly* removed from them because you didn't write them. But on the way to judging your own work with a touch of impersonality, ask yourself:

1. Which of these would you read first?

2. Write clearly the reasons why it would be your choice.

3. Would you stay with it? Why?

4. What do you think you would get out of it?

Once you've made up your mind as to whether you've done something basically worthwhile, you study the remarks on the slip of paper if it isn't just a printed rejection slip. If it *is*—hang on to your faith (remember?). You plan to improve what you've done—even if you have to do it alone, don't you? If, however, there are any (even one or two) kind words, remember my friend of the nine tries and take heart.

If either an editor or a professor offers suggestions, try to follow them. No editor, unless you are deeply professional, is going to ask you outright to change a whole piece of work. But a little suggestion or two is a hint that he basically likes what you've done and if it were changed (as in those suggestions), he'll look at it again.

In any case, you try to improve it, in the light of your own attempted impersonal reading. Try to *stay* impersonal. This is fairly simple if you have put a period of time between that first hot draft and your cooler reading of weeks later.

Of course, ideally, you should set aside all hot first drafts and let them cool off in the darkness of a desk drawer for a while. It's hard to do at first, but it's a restraint which can be learned with further work.

The temptation is always to want a professional opinion. You want to see whether you've really hit your stride. You just can't seem to let it rest. I have many stories I wish that I had let rest. It took years in some cases until I cooled off and grew a little and could say what was to be said with more craft and subtlety. But the young ideas were good and deserved more craft.

Assignment

*Take those five sensory descriptions you wrote back in Chapter Five.
Study them carefully.
Try to improve them now that you have done more writing.*

EVERYTHING IS CHANGE

How do you manage to change anything that is already stamped in black and white?

You do it in *four* ways.

1. Cutting
2. Revising
3. Rewriting
4. Polishing

Exceptionally conscientious and careful authors make this part of their daily work. First thing every morning they read over the work of the day before. They improve it in every way they can—adding, subtracting, changing.

This accomplishes two things. It assures that a first draft is mighty close to a finished product. And second, it gets writers in the mood, the swing, to go ahead. No matter how harsh they are with themselves, they're bound to find something in the previous day's labor to take pride in—like golfers who cuss at their game all around the course, but hit such a beautiful ball on the eighteenth hole that they can't wait to try again.

"SCALPEL . . ."

I was lucky right in the beginning, because I learned a great truth. *There is no story written that is not better for the cutting.*

"Beauty's Right," that happy first sale, ran well over twelve thousand words.

I was new to the whole thing. I'd never read a book about writing, or taken a course of any kind. I just sat down and wrote my story, letting my love of words take me into whatever maze they wanted to and embellishing many phrases with lacy ruffles of description.

On top of that, my so-called short story (which should have been just *one* incident, as you know) covered a lifetime for its characters, or a big hunk of it. If I had known what I do now, "Beauty's Right" would have been my first novel.

Ladies' Home Journal cut *ten whole pages.* At about two hundred fifty words a typewritten page, that reduced the whole by almost three thousand words.

When the story was published a year later, I could not see where they had cut it! Without the original copy I couldn't find the difference. They had done such a fine job of taking out nonessential words, phrases, sentences, sometimes whole paragraphs that everything important to the story—the moods, the people, the action, the background—was retained intact.

This is an art done by skilled editors. But it is an art that, as years go by, all writers must learn. The chance of today's busy editors searching for the nugget of gold under a lot of word dust is pretty remote. You have to learn to clip and trim for yourself.

It takes a lot of discipline to write concisely, as you've most likely learned working along here. You can't seem to get a piece down to the allotted number of words. When you look at the finished first draft, you can't bear to part with a precious one of them.

An agent's solid advice was, "Write as long as you have to. Let it have full flow. Put it away for a day or so. Then be ruthless with yourself and cut it to the bone. Then you'll have a story."

This, in time, you must learn to do. Seventeen pages of a short story, or ten or eleven for an article, are not very much. Not if you have a lot of things to say, ideas and people and facts and ramifications to include. The short story or article, like poetry, is a difficult form.

But even with these shorter forms the cutting *must* be done.

THE OPERATION

Search for *single unnecessary words.* Pencil them out.

Look for *repetitious phrases,* gremlins that crop in most writers' unpublished works. Occasionally it's good to repeat for accent, for rhythm, but often it's unnecessary.

It's strange. You litter a whole page with little black or red lines and bugs. You read in between them. It seems as if you had managed to cut hundreds of words. When you count them, they add up to a handful.

So, with courage and industry, you march on to *whole sentences*. You *incorporate*—take two ideas, each in a separate sentence, and try to tie them into one phrase. Investigate each piece of dialogue. If it doesn't forward or explain or show—out it goes.

You'll eventually come up with a much shorter piece of work. And each time you think you've cut as much as possible, start over again and cut still more.

A word of caution.

The word *cut* means: *sever, gash, divide in parts, carve, mow,* and *dilute.* If you do any of these things to your script you have mutilated it. It must still run sweetly and smoothly. So check carefully for jerkiness after you've cut.

Cut also means to *trim, pare, reduce, shorten*—and most important—to *form, shape,* or *adorn by cutting,* such as a diamond or a garment.

This is what you aim for.

Assignment

Take the five-hundred-word article you wrote for Assignment A in Chapter Ten.

Cut it to three hundred words.

Keep the essentials, the meaning, the point and a good steady flow of words. But take out unnecessary words, then repetitious phrases. Incorporate sentences and see what you come up with.

In a way, the work we do is a piece of cloth, the best material we can afford. It is a diamond, rough and unshining. It should be your job, as well as your privilege, to shape and adorn it as best you can.

In my current class, kept small by design in my home so that we may devote maximum attention to each piece of writing as it grows, we recently made a fascinating discovery. (It's always amazing how, in the process of working together, new approaches keep cropping up, each of them of value to all of the class.)

One of the women wrote a pretty good book. It had only one fault. It was too bland for a full-length mystery. She's a kindly, gentle person and this book seemed to evade her "killer instinct."

"It would make a good short story, or a one-shot small novel in *Hitchcock's Mystery Magazine* or *Ellery Queen*," one of the others said.

From the top of my head I suggested, "Why don't you go through it and write down the narrative hook of each paragraph and bring them in to read to us?"

She did. You know, she has a real story—still needing to be cut a little, of course, and smoothed out in a few transitions. But a real story that hits all the high points sharply.

So, lo! We have a reverse and quite different kind of cutting if we ever want to salvage a long work.

And it serves a second purpose, too, as another writer discovered. She found that by copying just the narrative hooks in the book she was working on, she could keep the continuity straight, pinpoint exactly the places where the story began to slow, or get confused, or miss the point—an invaluable way to keep track of logical progression and when and where it succeeds or fails.

There is one thing you can do to improve your efficiency in cutting and to see how it is managed by experts.

Buy *Reader's Digest*. Pick from the contents one article that is a reprint from another well-known magazine. Usually the issue date of the original is there with the article. Look up that issue in any library. Sit down with the two side-by-side.

You'll be astounded at the neatness with which one was changed into the other. You might ask yourself, "Which is the better, the easier, the clearer, to read?"

VISION AND REVISION

Once you've cut that article, or that new story, you begin to *revise*.

Revise has its own precise definition, too. It means: to look at, or over again, in order to correct or improve; to make a new, improved, or up-to-date version of a piece of writing.

I can give you no better example of revision than one right within this book. It proves you're never too old to learn. And writing dexterity doesn't mean that you can't fool yourself completely.

When I wrote the chapter about idea to theme to narrative hook, I just let myself go. I started out with narrative hooks, bounced over to getting started in the wrong direction, gave a personal example, switched over to theme with examples, back to narrative hooks with quotes, hopped backward to ideas, talked about an idea book, back again to narrative hooks, then five examples, to idea book again, to theme, to practicing narrative hooks, to examples of students' hooks, showed how to use newspaper questions with hooks, gave tests to try yourself, quoted more of my own starters.

After which, smug and certain of success when the book was finished, I sent it to my agent. He wrote:

> Although it begins rather abruptly with the mention of the narrative hook, there is then quite a bit of diffusion, to us confusing, a section of several pages until we get the connection between narrative hook (which is not mentioned again for some pages) and the various other subjects you mention—theme, idea book. It's difficult for us to know just what you are trying to get at in this chapter; there are so many ideas thrown in without being developed or connected, that we were quite confused. There are literally pages that can be taken out since the thing really gets underway on the tenth page, when it becomes clear what the relationship is between theme and narrative hook. The examples used here do not clarify the points, and that may be because these points are not made clearly, in a step-by-step progression.

Reading the chapter over I admired his patience and restraint.

If you will turn back to the chapter How Do You Really Start?, you can see what was done in revision.

HOW TO DO IT

To *revise* you must first of all know exactly what you want to include in the work. To accomplish this you make an outline, *a reminder*. This is to ensure if you went astray the first time, you'll stay close to home from now on.

Then you number your paragraphs: 1, 2, 3, 4.

You'll find that you really don't want to say anything too vitally different. What you want is to move it along in logical succession. You want to switch paragraphs. You want to exchange places like musical chairs. Any good revise, like the game, ends with one "paragraph-player" or more left over and out. It doesn't matter. That overweening text is cut a little more.

With your paragraphs numbered, you now begin to label the theme of each one. Or of a group of them that includes a single idea. Do this with pen or pencil between paragraphs. This way you section your work, which in turn helps you discover the exact point where you began to go wrong.

Next, you *ask questions of yourself*—and of each paragraph. Where is the gap between what you meant to say and what you really wrote? Is each sentence, each paragraph necessary? Would it, if it is, be better toward the end of the piece, the beginning, or anywhere else?

Is there an *important point* in any of the paragraphs that was so clear in your mind that you skipped over it and didn't give it its full value?

Read your beginning again and again. Is it the best narrative hook you can possibly write? Try others.

See if you have built up to that snarled point, which can be called the climax, the denouement, the second-act curtain. *All* writing, fiction or nonfiction, has this.

Follow each paragraph, not only for the way you phrased your idea, but ask if each forwards the action toward that high point. In an article this is the reason you wrote it in the first place and must be crystal clear—even more so in a short story.

There are people in both articles and fiction. Paragraph by paragraph, check each character. Ask, "Is he necessary? Does he come out in clear colors? Is he detailed and alive? A real person, for reader identification or interest?

Articles and stories both have dialogue. Read it aloud, for your own ears. Whether you are quoting figures given by the principal of a high school, or a highly charged fictional love scene, your people must really talk, as they would in real life.

When you have accomplished all this, and the slip of paper is scattered with notes, as is the story itself—get up and go take a walk. Or play some ball. Or bridge. Or read a book. You will be tense and irritable by this time. Don't blame yourself. Reworking is, without a doubt, frustrating, nerve-racking, and difficult. But you'll also find yourself pleased, even exhilarated, as if you had snipped from your personal physical self some weight you really didn't need.

Assignment

Take your five-hundred-word article and check it through the above methods and questions.

Shuffle and change until it is better in every way you can possibly see.

Remember, you are only renumbering and re-planning at this stage.

GET IT RIGHT—REWRITE

Now—your work is *out*. It is *revised*. This time you *rewrite*.

Rewriting is self-explanatory. It's more pleasant, too. It means to write again, to put into form for publication. Your paragraphs are numbered and in a different, better order, the precise way you want the finished work to be. Examine them once more.

Ask one probing question: "Could I have said it better?"

Apply this question to every sentence. Simpler? Fresher? More alive? Clearer? More natural? Does it flow? Characters sharp?

There are times when, in that beautiful rare glow of inspiration and spontaneous writing, you'll say exactly what you want to in the best manner possible. Rejoice! Most of the time there is a twist of phrase, a better adjective, even a richer bit of thought that will improve your work and make it publishable.

GET TO IT

A cub reporter on an evening newspaper learns a lot about rewriting. Each morning when he comes to his desk, along with the obituaries phoned in or clipped from the morning daily of his competitor, there will be a little pile of items from that same competitor. They are there for the cub to "rewrite."

This means that none of them is important enough to be covered by a more experienced reporter, or extended. They are newsy, however, and need to be included in the evening edition. The cub calls those involved, checks for accuracy. Then he spends many a frayed day trying to change them around. Cutting, revising, completely rewriting or rephrasing them. The point? To make them seem original, fresh, and fuller in the evening edition.

A cub holds his job by learning to do this well and often moves upward because he does.

You can learn to sell stories by learning to do this. It is the sign of a true professional that he's never quite satisfied with his product—whether cosmetics, electronics, or detergents. It's always the "New Improved" on television commercials. It must be the new, improved on everything that comes from your mind to paper.

Assignment

Clip five news stories from a daily newspaper.

Rewrite them, omitting no detail, so that they say the same thing in a new way.

Read these paragraphs thoughtfully, then do the assignment at their end:

> In the beginning there were three of us. Actually, of course, there still are. But it seems *more* three, looking back on it, in the beginning.
>
> People used to call us the Pretty One, the Sweet One, and the Smart One.
>
> It's not easy to know exactly where to start. There was a brown house. It was on Sixth Street, on the East Side, set back from the road. Which was just as well, for the trolleys racketed along there, and Mama was forever stewing for fear we'd get run over.
>
> Mama. She always used to call us, "My three little women," because she'd read Louisa May Alcott's *Little Women* eleven times by the time she was eleven. I think she would have liked it if we had called her "Marmee," although when I got old enough to read the classic myself I couldn't see any resemblances between her and the gentle, sugary-speaking woman who glided in and out among her girls.
>
> We were like Little Women, in that our father was away. He wasn't dead or a missing person or anything like that. But in effect he might just as

well have been. Our father was a traveling salesman.

When he was home, the atmosphere changed
mightily. We tiptoed so he could sleep and minded
our manners. He always looked dapper and
smelled of train smoke when he first came home,
and he brought us presents. He had a way of smil-
ing under his little black mustache as if he were real
proud of having fathered us but didn't quite know
how it had happened to a gay old dog like him. The
soul of a bachelor, I guess you'd say.

He couldn't have been a very good salesman, or
else a great deal of the money went to maintain him
in his outside activities. Mama never had very
much to do with. What she had she used wisely.
We looked as nice as anybody, and reveled in her
brown beef stews, chicken pies, and vegetable
soup. We grew up hardly ever sick.

Back of the house was a trellis. It was no ordi-
nary trellis. It was as long as the backyard, which
was very long and narrow. Spaced along the trellis, in recesses, were wooden seats, gray and worn
smooth by much sitting over a period of years. The
sides and top of the trellis were completely covered
with grapevines. In the winter, bare and as brown
as the wooden seats, they would clack and clap in
the wind. In the spring and summer, the buds
came, the leaves, and, finally, the grapes.

All I have to do to this day is close my eyes and
sniff and I can smell that rich purple smell and feel
the sort of snowy dust that frosts an individual
grape, and the pearlike touch it has against your
fingers. The way, when put to your lips and
squeezed, the slippery heart of it slithers against
your tongue and starts the juices under it, until
you are left with only the seeds to crunch and spit
out.

Assignment

Take your time on this assignment. If you do it well it's going to advance you enormously in your own work.

1. Rewrite, to the very best of your ability, the above example.

2. Considering the points made previously about cutting—cut your rewrite as much as you can and still keep all pertinent information.

MAKE IT SHINE: POLISH

This is the extra-super-special touch. It is a little indefinite but it's the time you take *after* you are absolutely sure you've done the best you can.

You take time to see if you and Webster agree that polish means to "finish by perfecting touches" or to "transform by polishing" or to "add luster." It isn't difficult to do. All the hard work has now been done. But, like the wax buffed on a clean kitchen floor, it's the extra gleam that makes the whole thing shine. Dream on your finished product a little to see if you can rub it in that extra way.

Whether there are only a few paragraphs in your desk drawer at the moment or half a dozen unfinished stories and articles—ones that pulled poor grades and sharp criticism—go to them. Pull them out. Cut them. Revise them. Rewrite them. Polish them.

One thing can be guaranteed. Not only will they be better when you've made those improvements; but you'll be a mile ahead as a writer. You'll be able not only to create—but to spot any technical weakness in your creation and repair it.

Afterword

If the pages in this book were one great long lecture—or a series of lectures—on writing, this is the place where I would stop and say, "Go thou and do likewise!" And then, "Any questions?"

The question period after any public talk is always interesting and often rewarding, once it gets rolling. It takes the speaker down from the podium and into the audience. The prepared and careful statements of the speech itself are discarded for "talking off the cuff" and open discussion. This session covers the odds and ends that the speaker didn't think to include.

You will have questions. Something important to you probably wasn't included in this book. Certain ones are always asked whenever an author speaks at a writers' conference, a college reading week, or just an author's meeting.

The first of them for some reason or other, is almost always, "Do I need an agent?" and "How did you get an agent?"

After that first sale of "Beauty's Right" every day I sat down at the typewriter I was horribly aware of the fact. *Ladies' Home Journal*, for pity's sake! When I quit my job to write, I was geared for a five-year haul of learning how-to. The immediate sale threw me into a state of shock from which I never would have recovered if it hadn't been for an agent.

One day, caught in the fear that grabbed my fingers every time I tried to write another story, I picked up a magazine. In it there was a copy of a short-short story published by *Collier's*. It showed the editor's changes. There was also a short letter from an agent named Sydney Sanders, giving permission to reprint the story.

Now understand that this experience with an agent was unique with me, and a symbol of a long time ago. Agents today would blow their stacks if their names were printed in such a magazine, as if they were advertising for unknown authors to besiege them with mail. Also today's agents do not handle short pieces as they used to. They would be more accessible at writers' conferences or, perhaps by a writer who had some long piece in progress. But I was fortunate at the time.

I wrote to him. I heard from him. With care he had checked with the *Journal* to find out what they thought of my potential. He said he would take me, no written contract, we could ditch each other whenever either of us wanted to (heaven forbid) and he told me to get to work.

With that letter—and that command—the dam began to loosen. The thing I learned, in this battle of the story and I, is that agents are great. Most of them. But they are *not* miracle workers. In no case, not ever and no matter how long you write, can they sell a story that isn't right. True for yesterday's markets—even more so for today's.

Stories from agents do get a prompter reading than ones sent in cold. But in the beginning you do not need an agent. A good story will find a place for itself and you cannot sell a bad story through the best agent in the world.

More importantly, I would not be writing today if it hadn't been for Sydney Sanders. He didn't try to teach me. He just kept me going. He sent back stories with caustic comments. He kept them and tried to sell them. He sometimes accomplished this with a story that he despised. He took care of foreign rights. He wrote me regularly. With only one sale behind me, one story published, that man sent faith to me.

It is my hope, of course, that this book may do something of the same for you.

THE BIGGEST STUMBLING BLOCK

Question: How do I keep from getting "blocked" when I try to write?

That is one cure everybody wants to know after a writers' talk. Writer's block strikes all writers—and I am no exception. I was so frightened after that first sale. I put on a cloak, somehow, every time I sat down at the typewriter.

"Now," I said to myself (and most beginners say the same thing) "I am no longer John Doe. I am an author and I am going to *write!*"

I saw the word that way, in italics with an exclamation point. In the process I put up an immediate barrier.

Writing is not something set apart from the everyday world and personal experience. Writing is an *extension* of yourself, just as the typewriter keys almost become part of your fingertips. You will never get a free, natural, honest flow if you think of yourself as a *writer* while you are writing.

You think of yourself, instead, as a channel, through which all of the strange, lovely, sad, and sometimes great, things of life can move. You put yourself, and your own personality, away somewhere, and you become those of whom you think.

This can be fun, as well as removing all self-consciousness from your work.

WHAT'S THE BIG IDEA?

"Where do you get your ideas?" they ask at a question session.

The sources are as varied as the people who try to write. Some get ideas from observing varied backgrounds. Others from a gimmick plot. Others from a phrase that sets them thinking. It goes on, well up into the lucky ones who can travel from place to place, soaking up all of those things together.

For me, because I have had to stay put, all ideas have started with people themselves, people around me or "people close to me." The turn of a head, a way of speaking, the expression of the eyes, a sentence that hints of a hidden problem—they set the imagination running. The first thing I know, there's a story in the making.

STOPPED SHORT

Because I have published only five books and have written numerous short stories and articles, there is invariably the question, "Why do you stay so closely to short stories?"

The answer is simple. Because I am a woman.

Being a woman writer poses very definite problems. Sometimes at one of those book and author deals, I look at the men and listen to them, and hear how they put in eight hours a day, every day without fail, and turn out a book every other year, or oftener. I drool to be a male writer for five or ten years.

I picture them at home in some far, hushed room, with their wives answering all phone calls, doorbells, taking care of plumbers, carpenters, gardeners, cleaning women, ironing shirts, preparing meals, serving them a light lunch at the middle of the day after timidly knocking on the door. Or perhaps retreating hastily when snarled at.

I consider how protected the men are, how uninterrupted their work can be, and I know why I write short pieces primarily.

It is because you can keep a short piece in your head. You find out how it's going to end, and you go about the business of making the beds, mopping the kitchen, baking the cakes, fixing the dinner, and you think about writing all the time.

You can write a short story or article fifteen minutes at a time, believe it or not, and be interrupted and go back to it, and rush to get things done so that you'll have another fifteen minutes free.

Actually, now that I think of it, you can write a novel the same way. A little at a time. Yes, now that I think of it—I did exactly that. With an ill mother, an eight-year-old son who had to be toted back and forth to school, piano lessons, scouts, and a husband who loved a hot dinner when he got home.

But, to tell the truth, I did it because I'd learned to work a scene at a time with short stories.

And the story gets finished.

WHY WRITE?

Beginners, listening to an established writer, always seem to ask the question, "How did you get started? Why are you writing?"

This is a hard one to answer. Why do I write? I know why I wrote in the first place and it is worlds apart from why I write now.

I wrote in the first place because I came out of college with a freshly printed bachelor of music degree in voice, right at the tag end of the Depression. Nobody wanted to hear an amateur mezzo-soprano for free, not to mention paying a five dollar fee.

So I managed a menial job on a newspaper and wrote my way to woman's editor. I wrote to make a living. I kept on writing for radio as continuity director for the same reason.

But always and always the dream was in me. Someday I would quit. Someday, because words had eaten themselves into my mind by then, I would write a full complete whole story all in one piece.

Believe it or not, this took almost ten years of my life.

Now, after all of those years, I write—not for money, fame, glory—but because I *have to*. I don't have any choice about it. Perhaps I didn't have from the beginning.

It isn't a case of a great exultant and glorious feeling derived from self-expression on paper. Although there are rare moments when that is true. It's more—and it's less.

It's a negative thing in some ways. I am more miserable (and more miserable to get along with) when I am not writing than when I am. The only way to take care of a mosquito bite, if you don't have any lotion to soothe it, is to scratch it. The only way to take care of the need to write—is to *write*. Every author I know feels this way.

That is all of the questions I can remember to ask. And all of the questions I have, offhand.

But thank you for being with me—for taking this course—and reading to the end of this book. I have enjoyed the inventory, the review, the simplicity of our writing together. I hope that you have, too. I hope that you are ready to settle down to this exciting creative activity.

I wish you well.

Index

Other Books of Interest

General Writing Books

Beginning Writer's Answer Book, edited by Polking and Bloss, $14.95
Getting the Words Right: How to Revise, Edit and Rewrite, by Theodore A. Rees Cheney $13.95
How to Become a Bestselling Author, by Stan Corwin, $14.95
How to Get Started in Writing, by Peggy Teeters $10.95
International Writers' & Artists' Yearbook, (paper) $10.95
Law and the Writer, edited by Polking and Meranus (paper) $7.95
Make Every Word Count, by Gary Provost (paper) $7.95
Teach Yourself to Write, by Evelyn A. Stenbock $12.95
Treasury of Tips for Writers, edited by Marvin Weisbord (paper) $6.95
Writer's Encyclopedia, edited by Kirk Polking $19.95
Writer's Market, edited by Bernadine Clark $18.95
Writer's Resource Guide, edited by Bernadine Clark $16.95
Writing for the Joy of It, by Leonard Knott $11.95
Writing From the Inside Out, by Charlotte Edwards (paper) $9.95

Magazine/News Writing

Complete Guide to Marketing Magazine Articles, by Duane Newcomb $9.95
Complete Guide to Writing Nonfiction, by the American Society of Journalists & Authors, edited by Glen Evans $24.95
Craft of Interviewing, by John Brady $9.95
Magazine Writing: The Inside Angle, by Art Spikol $12.95
Magazine Writing Today, by Jerome E. Kelley $10.95
Newsthinking: The Secret of Great Newswriting, by Bob Baker $11.95
1001 Article Ideas, by Frank A. Dickson $10.95
Stalking the Feature Story, by William Ruehlmann $9.95
Write On Target, by Connie Emerson $12.95
Writing and Selling Non-Fiction, by Hayes B. Jacobs $12.95

Fiction Writing

Creating Short Fiction, by Damon Knight $11.95
Fiction Is Folks: How to Create Unforgettable Characters, by Robert Newton Peck $11.95
Fiction Writer's Help Book, by Maxine Rock $12.95
Fiction Writer's Market, edited by Jean Fredette $17.95
Handbook of Short Story Writing, by Dickson and Smythe (paper) $6.95
How to Write Best-Selling Fiction, by Dean R. Koontz $13.95
How to Write Short Stories that Sell, by Louise Boggess (paper) $7.95
One Way to Write Your Novel, by Dick Perry (paper) $6.95
Secrets of Successful Fiction, by Robert Newton Peck $8.95
Writing Romance Fiction—For Love And Money, by Helene Schellenberg Barnhart $14.95
Writing the Novel: From Plot to Print, by Lawrence Block $10.95

Special Interest Writing Books

Cartoonist's & Gag Writer's Handbook, by Jack Markow (paper) $9.95
The Children's Picture Book: How to Write It, How to Sell It, by Ellen E. M. Roberts $17.95

Complete Book of Scriptwriting, by J. Michael Straczynski $14.95

Complete Guide to Greeting Card Writing, edited by Larry Sandman (paper) $7.95

Complete Guide to Writing Software User Manuals, by Brad McGehee (paper) $14.95

Confession Writer's Handbook, by Florence K. Palmer. Revised by Marguerite McClain $9.95

Guide to Greeting Card Writing, edited by Larry Sandman $10.95

How to Make Money Writing . . . Fillers, by Connie Emerson $12.95

How to Write a Cookbook and Get It Published, by Sara Pitzer, $15.95

How to Write a Play, by Raymond Hull $13.95

How to Write and Sell Your Personal Experiences, by Lois Duncan $10.95

How to Write and Sell (Your Sense of) Humor, by Gene Perret $12.95

How to Write "How-To" Books and Articles, by Raymond Hull (paper) $8.95

Mystery Writer's Handbook, edited by Lawrence Treat (paper) $8.95

Poet and the Poem, revised edition by Judson Jerome $13.95

Poet's Handbook, by Judson Jerome $11.95

Programmer's Market, edited by Brad McGehee (paper) $16.95

Sell Copy, by Webster Kuswa $11.95

Successful Outdoor Writing, by Jack Samson $11.95

Travel Writer's Handbook, by Louise Zobel (paper) $8.95

TV Scriptwriter's Handbook, by Alfred Brenner $12.95

Writing and Selling Science Fiction, by Science Fiction Writers of America (paper) $7.95

Writing for Children & Teenagers, by Lee Wyndham. Revised by Arnold Madison $11.95

Writing for Regional Publications, by Brian Vachon $11.95

Writing to Inspire, by Gentz, Roddy, et al $14.95

The Writing Business

Complete Handbook for Freelance Writers, by Kay Cassill $14.95

Freelance Jobs for Writers, edited by Kirk Polking (paper) $7.95

How to Be a Successful Housewife/Writer, by Elaine Fantle Shimberg $10.95

How You Can Make $20,000 a Year Writing, by Nancy Hanson (paper) $6.95

Profitable Part-time/Full-time Freelancing, by Clair Rees $10.95

The Writer's Survival Guide: How to Cope with Rejection, Success and 99 Other Hang-Ups of the Writing Life, by Jean and Veryl Rosenbaum $12.95

To order directly from the publisher, include $1.50 postage and handling for 1 book and 50¢ for each additional book. Allow 30 days for delivery.

Writer's Digest Books, Department B
9933 Alliance Road, Cincinnati OH 45242
Prices subject to change without notice.